Also by the author

THE LAW OF FALLING BODIES

SMALL CLAIMS

Half

BY JILL CIMENT

a Life

ANCHOR BOOKS
A Division of Random House, Inc.
New York

ANCHOR BOOKS EDITION

Copyright © 1996 by Jill Ciment

Anchor Books and colophon are registered trademarks of Random House, Inc.

Library of Congress Cataloging-in-Publication Data

Ciment, Jill, 1953–
Half a life / by Jill Ciment.
p. cm.
1. Ciment, Jill—Childhood and youth.   2. Women
authors, American—20th century—Biography.
3. Children of the mentally ill—California—
Los Angeles—Biography.   4. Los Angeles
(Calif.)—Social life and customs.
5. Family—California—Los Angeles.
I. Title.
[PS3553.I45Z465   1997]
813'.54—dc21
[B]   97-10815
CIP

ISBN 978-0-385-48891-4

Book design by Lauren Dong

www.anchorbooks.com

Printed in the United States of America
BVG 01

FOR ARNOLD

The author wishes to thank
the National Endowment for the Arts and
the Altos de Chavón Foundation
for their generous support.

PART

ONE

Once a friend told me about a strange-looking man who gave the stock and futures report on an obscure cable channel. My friend thought he must have been chosen as a joke by some black-humored station manager. The man stammered, never made eye contact with the viewer (instead, he stared at a remote point in a generic living room), and often seemed on the verge of panic. He had the same last name as I did and she wondered if he could be a distant relative.

Blinking, sitting on the edge of her sofa, I watched my father. I hadn't seen him in years. My father has always looked, to me at least, like a child's drawing of an adult—a gigantic balloon tethered to the world by spindly sticks. He had not changed. His cheeks were enormous. His top lip perspired. His eyes registered no emotion save fear. I wondered who out there in television land was entrusting him with their life savings.

Then, closing my eyes for a moment, I felt something inside me break.

My father stopped living with us when I was fourteen. During our last months together, he spent the majority of his time gardening—eighteen, sometimes twenty hours at a stretch, a hoe in one hand, a flashlight in the other. He couldn't understand why his children didn't join him, and would stand on the brick patio, bellowing our names. His voice would crash through my dreams. And find me. In rooms I never visited during wakefulness.

When I opened my eyes, he was, full-screen, calling out the rock-hard elements of the world—gold up, silver down, platinum holding steady. And then he called out the staples—wheat, corn, eggs, rye . . .

His hands were trembling; his eyebrows looked exactly like mine.

———†———

I'd stumbled upon him twice before during our long hiatus, each time more disconcerting than the last.

Profiled in *Time* magazine as the quintessential type A personality, he was photographed on a doctor's table, feet facing camera. If my brothers hadn't shown me the picture, I probably wouldn't have recognized him (he was even more obese than I remembered). For some reason, it was the soles of those bare feet that walked my dreams for weeks afterward.

The other time took place in a college library, as I was leafing through an art magazine. I was glancing at a photo essay on Los Angeles. It wasn't a particularly interesting spread. The ideas were pedestrian, the images manipulative, the captions clichéd. A full-color snap of a Jack in the Box restaurant clown.

"LA Eats," the caption read. An overhead view of a colossal traffic jam: "The World Stops." Then I saw, at point-blank range, my father's apartment building, the Montego Arms, with his lime green Pinto out front. I could read the license plate, see a box of tissues on the dash. In those years, low-cost furnished apartments in LA were coated with glowing stucco to break the monotony of their bivouac style. The Arms was no exception. It stood sunstruck in the noon glare. The shadows under my father's tires were purple. Through two open windows, I could see two orange sofas facing two blank TVs. The caption read, "The Living Dead."

My mother, no great fan of my father, says he wasn't always so peculiar. While we lived in Montreal, checked by the restraints of his extended family, he was—if not normal—passable. He had a business (his father's hat store), a gang of old college friends, a semiattached house, a wife and three children. Still relatively thin and handsome in those days, he kept up a semblance of middle-class decorum—an Ivy League cut for his thinning black hair, a dark suit, and wing tips. He even let my mother trim his massive, unruly eyebrows. Though he disliked being touched and rarely showed affection, he sometimes let us kids climb onto his back. Only after we lit out for California did things go awry.

The year was 1964. Whenever I envision that journey, a couple of images come to mind. The first was fed to me by my mother and holds within its aura the power and pull of her imagination. It's a picture of my father, and within him, some vital aspect of his being—his moral fiber, a stitch that fastens him to reality—somehow getting snagged on our front porch in Montreal so that as we roll across the country, inch by foot by yard, he slowly comes undone.

The second is wholly my own and takes place in a boggy motel room, just outside of Needles. It's our last night on the road. The air is stultifying. My parents, two brothers, and I are crammed into one room—a tiny double with three creaky cots. No one can sleep. By the way my father is lying there, curled on his side, I can tell he's worried. I can tell because I'm worried, too. This is what my father and I have in common. We can't stop worrying. My mother worries as well, but she has the enviable capacity to get her fretting done lickety-split. My father and I are brooders. All night long, our obsessions don't quit; they go around and around, like socks in a washing machine.

Tonight I'm worried about moving to Los Angeles and not being able to shed my old, tiresome personality for the new one I've planned—a carefree California preteen.

My father is worried about money. I know, because all his worries are variations on a theme. As some people are terrified of spiders or heights or windowless rooms, my father is terrified of spending money. And he's frightened of all objects that have to be replaced or repaired by spending money. And, I believe, he's terrified of money itself, of its thin, friable surface. And, I know, he's terrified of my brothers and me for outgrowing our shoes, for whining for comic books and candy bars.

My mother, often repelled by the touch of my father, is holding on to her narrow margin of mattress and fantasizing about a sunnier future.

And I have an unbearable feeling that if all our wishes were suddenly granted, I'd obliterate the very essence of my being, my father would dream his children away, my mother would have my father disappear, so that when the maid trundled in with her linen cart the next morning, she'd find the beds slept in, but empty.

———†———

We got to LA the day the hills went up in flames. The fire burned for days. It rampaged down canyons, sparing one mansion, ravaging another. For some reason, this conflagration completely satisfied my fantasies about California—it had unspeakable beauty, weeping movie stars, Technicolor flames.

On TV, in the sweltering motel where we lived until my father found work, I watched a palm burn in Zsa Zsa Gabor's backyard; it burned like torched hair. Whole afternoons, my mother, brothers, and I sat spellbound, waiting to see if Burt Lancaster's roof would catch fire, if Red Skelton would lose his poolside cabana.

As soon as the blazes were quelled and the police barricades came down, my family joined the hordes to gawk. In head-to-toe traffic, we rubbernecked our way past scorched pillars that flanked charred driveways that led to melted staircases spiraling up into ash. On one tiered plot, an enormous glass wall stood alone in its coal black frame, dividing nothing from nothing. Only the swimming pools lay intact, turquoise and sparkling, as though beckoning us to take a dip in hell.

I couldn't get enough of it. Had I been given the option, we'd have returned weekend after weekend. Even my father seemed transfixed. Why the allure of charred ruins? The joy of someone else's disaster? The fact that even money and fame can't save you? Probably, but something else, too. While we motored past such total wreckage, the smell of smoke in our hair, I felt carefree. Since we'd arrived in LA, we'd harbored a tension that was enormous, even for us. You could see it in our gestures, hear it in the ping of our forks as we ate Van de Kamp's take-out dinners in front of the TV. But on nights after we drove by the devastation, we slept like the dead, my parents flopped on a single bed, my brothers and I wedged into cots.

The motel was cramped and getting expensive. The walls were paper-thin. People slammed doors all night long. One elderly neighbor compulsively flushed his toilet. We had to find a permanent home.

LA is divided by the Santa Monica Mountains, three-thousand-foot peaks that snake between the ocean and the desert valleys, between opulence and hardscrabble tract houses, between salty mists and air that is so dry the sweat on your skin just flashes away to nothing. After the fire, whenever I saw a TV helicopter shot of the city, it looked as if someone had drawn a charcoal line down the center to divide Them from Us, Rich from Poor, Here from There. To save money and because somewhere in the back of my father's head was the half-baked dream of becoming a pioneer, he opted for the valley.

Our real estate broker had once been a bit player on the old *Superman* series. I recognized him immediately. He stood six foot three and had ears gnarled as roots. He played the thug who always showed up with the green bar of Kryptonite to rob Superman of his otherworldly powers. When I got him to autograph the back of my comic book, I felt as if I'd truly arrived.

He showed us tract houses on the outer fringes of the San Fernando Valley, subdivisions with names like Sunburst and Cherry Tree Hills (there were no hills, no trees, let alone cherries). Most of the land had been stolen from the desert, the yards laced with chemicals to lure crabgrass out of the sandy soil. Once in awhile, a contractor would go bust, after having sold only one or two homes. These divisions afforded the best deals. When we drove down their desolate cul-de-sacs, the two or three children that lived there would charge to the front window or chase our broker's station wagon with frenetic speed.

After weeks of indecision, our money dwindling fast, my parents finally settled on a ranch-style house in the dead center of the valley. While they signed the papers, the broker casually mentioned that where I sat, scrunched beside my mother at the built-in breakfast nook, was thirteen feet below sea level. Perhaps this accounted for the ear-ringing stillness, my sense of crackling calm. Our subdivision, Rancho del Sol, was almost five years old, ancient by local standards. Most of the neighbors had already erected six-foot cinder-block fences around their tiny properties. Cupping my ear to the hollow bricks, I could make out the dull thwacks of tetherballs, the pops of cap guns, the shrill squeals of children. Back east, only tiny shrubs divided the properties. Everyone knew one another. This was one of the reasons my mother wanted to emigrate. On humid summer Montreal evenings with the windows wide open, the Ehrenreichs, the Golds, the Richlers, the Hirshmans could all hear my father bellowing.

For the first couple of nights, between the stillness and the unfamiliar bed, I couldn't fall asleep. Most mornings, I tried to nap or poked around the backyard with my brothers until the heat became intolerable, until I flopped down on the brown lawn in a stupor. My limbs felt as weighted as sandbags. Sometimes it seemed as if, with no effort, I might sink into the soil, into dirt that was so parched it would absorb anything.

Despite the heat, my mother unpacked boxes, eyeballed measurements, paced off rooms in her lavender felt slippers. (She was still trying to be a good housewife in those days. Only later would she hem my father's pants with a staple gun, take up my skirts with duct tape.) For her, any and all change was good. If the next hillock was a tad greener, even a dull pea green greener, she yearned to take off. In restaurants, she could barely enjoy her food for envy of what everyone else ordered.

She was thirty-three years old but looked twenty-three, with a lost, smoky gaze and flyaway hair she dyed in endless shades of blond. Even though my dad was only six years her senior, they were often mistaken for father and daughter.

By midafternoon, if she wasn't too tired, she took us on walks through the neighborhood. She wanted to orient us in case we got lost. She also wanted to see where in the world she'd wound up. In every direction, mountains scrambled out of the haze. Cars hurled down the boulevards. We met no one. We were the only people on foot. We donned rubber thongs and trod upon our own tiny shadows.

Despite the isolation, or perhaps because of it, my mother sensed possibilities. And I got caught up in her mood. As we walked along, she told us stories about soda jerks and movie ushers discovered by big-shot producers, a young mother who made zillions gambling her grocery allowance on uranium stocks, the local plumber who found oil under his backyard, men and women who went to bed paupers and woke up Vanderbilts. My father's distant cousin had emigrated here after the war and invested in land along a dirt strip that later became the Miracle Mile. Anything could happen.

When the sun reached its zenith and the sidewalk turned scalding, she herded us home and sat us in front of the swamp cooler. It came with the house. I'd never seen anything like it before, and never have since. The cooler's front looked like an old Chevy radiator filled to the brim with water; its back held a gigantic fan, with blades as long as baseball bats. When you turned it on, the floor and walls shook. Our sofa lay perpendicular to it and we sat in a row, our clothes flapping, our hair sticking straight out. I believe the cooler's wind gave my mother the sensation of going places. It certainly gave my brothers and me the pomp and thrill of a hurricane ride. And for the rest of the afternoon until my father came home, we shouted over its blast or crooned songs—"You've Lost That Lovin' Feeling," "Mama Said," "The Lion Sleeps Tonight" (I chanted the "wimoweh" chorus). Normally, I never let myself sing out loud (I am tone-deaf and find melody as mysterious as night). But in the roar of the swamp cooler, I sang along with the family, crooning from the depths of my soul.

Then my father pulled into the driveway. He wasn't doing too well. You could hear it in the tone of voice he used to call for my mother. He didn't call so much to find out her whereabouts as to express some baleful need. He had taken a job with Sears Roebuck, designing the circuitry for their lighting-fixture exhibits, the garish displays where chandeliers dangle beside pogo-stick pole lamps. Having studied to be an engineer, he found the work demeaning, the pay pitiful. He didn't get along

11

with his boss or his colleagues. He came home edgy. His edginess scared me—not for any violent quality, but because it was so doggedly mundane. Say one of us kids accidentally spilled a carton of milk during dinner. He became frantic, obsessing about the wasted milk. He thought of nothing but milk. He talked ceaselessly about the accident, asking us again and again how it could have happened. How could we have been so reckless? And when (to all our relief) he finally went to sleep, I know he dreamed of milk, aqueducts of milk, milk gone bad, soured by the sun, ending in drains. And for some reason, I woke up thirsty.

The house was pitch-black. I put my feet down to make sure the world was there, was flat. Then I padded out onto the patio. My older brother Jack must have heard me because a moment later, he shambled out in his striped pajamas. Next my mother appeared, carrying my little brother Tommy. She sat down on the brick parapet between Jack and me. The air was smoky. A new fire burned on the far side of the mountains. But from where we sat, in the bowl of the valley, it looked like it was burning in another world.

Every day one thousand new people poured into Los Angeles, harboring every possible pipe dream. I was no different.

When I entered junior high school that fall, I planned on jettisoning certain aspects of my personality along with my accent and mittens. Back home, I'd been a Goody Two-shoes obsessed with pleasing my elementary school teachers. If one of them yelled at me, I experienced the flush of humiliation as a painful rash.

I planned on becoming tougher and made a study of my new school's hierarchy. On top of the heap were girls who had already developed—not the beanpole kind who hunched over to avoid the janitor's brazen stare, but the busty ones who let their garters flash, donned white lipstick, and dated boys with cars.

On the next tier were girls who belonged to gangs—the Thunderbirds, Las Gatas, the Blades. They brandished hickeys, ratted their hair, snapped back at teachers, and smoked unfiltered Camels in the Quonset hut bathrooms. No one like them existed in Canada.

Several notches beneath them clustered girls who aspired to be girls who belonged to gangs. This was where I staked my claim. I was eleven years old, four foot ten, seventy-two pounds. The circumference of my knees was greater than my thighs. My only social attribute was that I could dance the James Brown. All I had were my ambitions.

And below me, hanging back against the schoolyard fence, milled the hordes—children for whom this caste system was insufferable. My brother Jack was among them. He spent the better part of his lunch period avoiding taunts and fistfights. A bright boy of thirteen, he knew enough to keep his Hebrew books brown-bagged and stashed in his locker. *Jew* was bandied around the yard as a verb. "You owe me a quarter! Don't try to jew me down!" One afternoon, I overheard a couple of Thunderbirds discussing why Jews don't believe in Jesus. Evidently, because he was only a poor carpenter.

I gathered up my books and said nothing. I knew nothing. I'd never even been inside a temple. My father was going to have Jack bar mitzvahed in the back of a storefront on a Wednesday morning to save money. Besides, I would have put up with almost anything to be accepted.

———†———

My crowd included the Kerkorian sisters, Julie and Nancy, two large Armenian girls who shared my aspirations. The year before, with the help of their fifteen-year-old sister Heather, they'd almost made it into the Blades. But Heather had to be shunted away for nine months because of a hush-hush medical condition and the sisters lost their foothold.

After school, with no place to go, we hung out in store parking lots, smoking cigarette butts chucked away by the shoppers. We couldn't go to Julie and Nancy's place because Mr. Kerkorian worked nights, slept mornings, then drank all afternoon. (Mrs. Kerkorian had run away with the Roto-Rooter man.) My house was out of the question because my father got off work at four, agitated and seething.

So mostly, we drifted in and out of dime stores, pocketing an occasional lipstick tube. When we weren't "shopping," we were plotting how to curry favor with the tougher girls. The only gang kind enough to talk to me was Las Gatas. But they were all Chicanas, and only Chicanas could join. Julie and Nancy loathed Mexicans. Both dark girls, they were often mistaken for being Latina and they refuted these blunders with a ferocity that left me speechless.

In the late afternoons, as soon Mr. Kerkorian swerved off to work, we hurried back to Julie and Nancy's house to gloat over our booty of lipsticks—Ripe Rose, Fuchsia Nights, Lady Pink, Firecracker Red. Vying for a spot in front of their mother's vanity mirror, we painted our pursed and open lips. Then, making loud smooching sounds, we kissed tissues, not just to blot off the excess color but also, I think, to see our mark on the world. We examined these smudges endlessly. Next, we pilfered Heather's closet for fishnet stockings and spiked heels, squeezed into our short shorts, stuffed our trainer bras with cotton balls, and hit the boulevards. We took truck routes, sashaying along the curb. The idea was to elicit truckers' wolf whistles. In the wake of semis, we bumped bony hips and goaded one another on. If a trucker did whistle, however, or made lewd hooting sounds or licentiously wagged his tongue, we pretended to gag. But secretly, we harbored the hope that someday we might be desired.

One afternoon, dressed in full regalia—Kewpie-doll lips, lamé tube tops, and cotton balls—we passed the schoolyard. It was late fall. The Santa Ana was gusting. Silver candy wrappers flapped and jackknifed against the cyclone fence. Standing by the drinking fountain, a clump of Las Gatas girls were smoking cigarettes, leaving fire falls of blowing ash. Maria, the youngest, glanced over at us (we knew one another from class), did a double take, and laughed. It wasn't a cruel laugh, just a burst of incredulity at our getups.

I was inclined to smile back, but Julie stopped me.

She mumbled something under her breath, then nudged Nancy and me through the gate. She marched us across the playground, making as if she was going to get a drink of water. The Las Gatas girls shifted out of our way. The fountain was choked with cigarette butts, gum wads, and sand. I could see our reflection in the spigot—fish-eyed, jittery, and painted.

Letting loose an arc of water, Julie just stared at it and sighed:

"I'm sure I'm going to drink from the same fountain that beaners use."

The first blow struck her on the back of the neck. I heard her tooth crack against the spigot (the same tooth that usually held a smudge of Lady Pink). Then a flurry of fists rained on her back and shoulders. Bloodied and stunned, she threw punches and screamed gibberish. Nancy screamed in unison. I backed up in Heather's high heels (no easy feat) and made for the fence. I didn't look back. I simply fished the cotton balls out of my unwieldy bra, kicked off the shoes, wrapped my fingers around the wire mesh and hoisted myself to safety.

———†———

When the Kerkorian sisters became too much for me, I hung out with the Yamamoto sisters, Shirley and Lynn, two shy girls who actually looked up to me. They wore identical bowl haircuts and spoke so softly that I had to stop popping my gum just to be able to hear them. When they weren't helping out in their family's gardening business, they studied ceaselessly, heads bowed over their wooden desks, over the slate gray cafeteria trays, over the long blond library tables. They won me no status on the schoolyard. What I liked about them was Mr. Yamamoto, a small, graceful man who doted on his daughters.

I honestly believed I had so much more personality than Shirley and Lynn combined that Mr. Yamamoto was pleased to have me around.

Poised on the hem of his driveway, I'd wait beside his daughters for him to come home, then watch in mute disbelief at the simple affections he'd lavish upon them.

On Saturdays, he took us bowling. Shirley and Lynn were completely inept at it. They always chose the lightest balls, then dropped them like millstones onto the polished lanes. I had to endure wasted minutes while their balls lackadaisically wobbled down the gutter. I was a crack shot. I could wipe out splits, hook the ball, explode the pins. But when Mr. Yamamoto gave out pointers, I queued up behind his daughters. With exquisite gentleness, he took hold of our arms, lightly cupping our elbows in his hand, and led us through backswings.

For hours afterward, I dwelled on his touch, not quite sure if the pleasure emanated from his fingertips or my longing.

———†———

I would have done anything to be desired. As it was, I shampooed my hair twice every night, then applied gobs of Dippity-Do to obliterate my unfashionable curls. I used the shape of my skull as a gigantic roller, an armature on which to mold my hopes, wrapping the sticky wet strands around and around, save for a clump of bangs and fringe of kiss curls. These I Scotch-taped flat against my forehead and cheeks. Sometimes during the night, tiny pimples appeared under the translucent tape. I had to sleep on my fists to keep bobby pins from stabbing me. Often I dreamed about the sheer weight of my head. My alarm clock trilled at six. By ten past, I was back in front of the mirror, raking out the Dippity-Do. When a comb could pass through it, I began teasing my hair. I tried to create a mass of rising thickness, like a soufflé, over which I brushed a smooth layer. Some of the tougher girls used balloons to create their colossal bouffants; the toughest kept razor blades hidden underneath. When I'd achieved whatever height I could that day, I began on my makeup, smearing on foundation, patting on blush, dabbing my pimples with pancake. I started my eyeliner just below the tear duct and swept it along, rising to a curlicue that aped a real eyelash. I repeated the same stroke on the underlid. I brushed on so many layers of mascara, I couldn't tell if it was the paint or exhaustion, but my eyelids felt as heavy as garage doors. For my outfit, I chose a tight mohair sweater, jersey dickey, and black vinyl hip-hugger miniskirt. I made sure my garters flashed. If a run began in my nylon stockings, I quashed it with a glob of red nail polish.

Finally, turning profile, then full-face, I studied the whole effect in the mirror.

I knew that some boys liked girls who dressed tough. Some boys liked girls with scrubbed skin. Some men liked girls in white crinoline or vinyl miniskirts or kneesocks or red bowling shirts. Somebody loves us all.

———†———

My mother saw my ache and worried about me. But mostly, she worried about Tommy and Jack. Tommy didn't like kindergarten and Jack wasn't making friends as easily as I. A shy, studious boy, Jack found the brutal rituals of the schoolyard intolerable, the coded slang of American pubescent bantering as mysterious as Sanskrit.

I worshiped him at home but avoided him at school because of his white socks, his ill-fitting slacks, his unruly cowlicks (two tornadoes of Brylcreem flanking his part). His passions were science and music. Inquisitive to the point of dreaminess, he built a makeshift laboratory in the garage and wrote songs on an acoustic guitar behind his locked bedroom door. At least twice a week, my father would pummel the door with his fists, screaming at Jack to earn his keep. My brother would strum louder. He dreamed of getting an electric guitar so he could write rock 'n' roll songs. I desparately wanted a bubble hairpiece to help me feel prettier.

My mother tried to buy us whatever she could afford to make us happy, but pleaded with us not to tell our father.

When she surprised Jack with a cherry red electric guitar, he had to pretend a neighbor gave it to him. When Tommy played with a new toy, he had to say he found it in a trash can. I posed less of a problem because my father rarely noticed me, let alone my new Woolworth hairpiece. All our clothes, an electric frying pan, new shoes, a microscope for Jack were, according to my mother, the generous gifts of others—neighbors even poorer than we were. Did my father believe her? Yes and no. He wasn't a fool, but at the same time, he was so petrified of spending money that he desperately wanted to believe her magnetism could get the indifferent world to rally to his aid, that she could convince *someone* to take care of *him*.

He had no friends. No one. The phone never rang for him. No one dropped by. He knew none of the neighbors. He didn't get along with any of his coworkers. Unwilling to shell out for lunch at the employee cafeteria, he ate alone at his desk from a brown-bag lunch my mother fixed him.

On Saturdays, we lived in trepidation of the mail. Weekdays, my mother opened it first, removed the monthly credit-card bills and shredded any evidence of what she'd bought—a wa-wa pedal for Jack's guitar, say, or an Etch-A-Sketch for Tommy. (My chore was to get rid of the carbon shreds by stuffing them into the neighbors' trash cans). On payday, she handed my father only the slips with the totals. He bellowed, but he had no proof of her purchases. Come the weekends, however, he could get to the bills first, and we all feared that possibility.

One Saturday, he discovered the payment plan for my brother's guitar. He grabbed Jack by his jersey dickey and pinned him to the garage floor, mashing his cheek against an oil slick.

Jack froze instantly. He was all spruced up for a band rehearsal. He'd joined a group called the Waves fashioned after the Beach Boys. They played the Top 40—"Wipeout," "In My Room"—and, at my insistence, wore matching outfits: white turtleneck dickeys, black slacks with silver piping, black collarless jackets, black socks. Determined not to bruise his hands or rip his new jacket, Jack tried to squirm his way out of my father's grasp.

My father sat down on top of him. "Lorraine!" he shouted for my mother. "Give me those credit cards. Give me those credit cards now or I'll kill the kid!" Then, bending over his son as if he were a conspirator, he whispered, "Is she trying to ruin me? Oh God, she's trying to ruin me. That's it, isn't it? She's trying to ruin me." He pressed his fingers to his temples and rocked back and forth as if his son weren't there, as if Jack weren't being flattened by his hefty, rolling weight. "Oh God, what am I going to do? What am I going to do?"

My mother rushed into the garage and pummeled and pinched my father's arms until Jack broke free. He tore off into his room, bolting the door behind him. My mother threw down a credit card, then walked to the end of the driveway, sat down on the dusty curb and wrapped her arms around her knees. Her blond hair looked vaguely iridescent in the noon glare. There wasn't a breeze anywhere. My father stayed in the garage, pacing back and forth, asking again and again why no one saw his point of view, why no one was ever on his side. I hung back in the stippled shadows of the breezeway, watching them both with a sense of unbearable sadness. Before me, they became a scared boy who had no friends and a girl who wished she was somewhere else.

S ometimes my mother slipped into my bed at night and curled up beside me. I was her confidante. Without meaning to, she told me more about my father than I wanted to know: how he wouldn't change his boxer shorts, how he skipped baths to save money on hot water, how he once yelled so loudly that the neighbors thought he'd killed us.

On Saturdays, she and I sat together on the brick patio, watching him through the gauzy dimensions of the screen door as he raged about minutiae or became so immobilized in front of the black-and-white Zenith that even now I can close my eyes and his TV ghost remains—a stout, balding silhouette haloed in blue cigar smoke.

I said I thought she should leave him. I said I didn't know why she had married him in the first place.

This wasn't true. By twelve, I had pieced together their story.

She was nineteen, on the rebound, and living in a fog. My father was considered a good catch—college-educated, the son of a successful businessman, the grandson of a rabbi. (My mother's family were tailors and small-time gamblers, lapsed Jews who ate ham and took cabs on Yom Kippur.) There were signs, plenty of warning signs; she just refused to see them. She had some cockamamy dream that her first love, a boy much poorer than my father, would rescue her at her wedding, Hollywood-fashion.

But the memory that knocked me breathless was that a neighbor of my father's, a widowed seamstress, had phoned my mother on the eve of her wedding to warn her not to marry him, saying that loud screaming poured from the Ciment household day and night, and my mother hadn't listened to her.

I said if she was going to leave him, she should do it on a Monday morning, maybe even this Monday morning. For some reason, I thought my father would be less upset about our disappearing if he had the full workweek to forget about us.

My mother tilted back her head and shut her eyes.

We'd been over this territory before, practically trampled it lifeless. After eight months in LA, any hope of sunny California improving my father's disposition was long gone.

She got up and scuffed across the yard, kicking a mud clod with her lavender slipper. She had eighty-six dollars squirreled away, three kids, no education, no skills, and she knew a total of eight people in the United States—a couple of neighborhood pals in the same predicament as she, five distant relatives of my father's who didn't return his calls, and one lavender-smelling aunt who did speak to us, but she also spoke to her parakeet.

To begin the arduous task of saving up for our escape, my mother took a part-time job selling clothes in a shopping mall. Her paychecks were piddling, her commissions dinky and sporadic. It didn't matter. We considered her job a practice run to see if she could make it on her own. Jack offered to baby-sit Tommy so that she could work Friday nights and weekends. If I didn't have homework (I constantly played hooky, so I rarely had homework), I tagged along with her. Like most of the other working mothers, she used the glass-enclosed shopping mall as a day camp. Throngs of adolescents drifted back and forth, palming occasional jawbreakers, then gumming up the display windows with their candied breath. The only rules were not to leave the shopping mall and not to let your mother's boss see you. Gangs formed. The older children robbed the younger ones, collaring them in the smoky lavatories.

My mother gave me a dollar per diem, which I hid in my shoe, budgeting my pennies with an exactitude I never applied in arithmetic. I allowed myself one chocolate bar, one bag of caramel popcorn, one hamburger teeming with freebies, and a small Coke that I slurped and savored until the stores closed. Sometimes, dazed by the aimlessness of it all, nauseous from the sweets, I waited for her by the fountain (a glycerin column of simulated water), feeling as if no other world existed but this one, no air that wasn't tinged with cheap sample perfume, no sun save for the tepid rays that filtered through the tinted mall glass.

Around seven, flushed from a last-minute sale, she joined me and we went over how much she had earned that day, how much we would have in a month, how much we would have in three months if, say, she doubled or tripled or—why not?—quintupled her commissions. By the time we glided onto the freeway, high on the wizardry of her mathematics, she had us flush, packed, and moving to Waikiki. From the way she talked about it, I pictured Hawaiian Punch flowing freely out of the taps there.

Then we pulled into our driveway. My father was either pacing the breezeway or weeding by moonlight, mumbling things we couldn't make out. My brothers were nowhere in sight. Through the open Dutch doors, we could see kitchen stools overturned or a glass shattered on the linoleum. One night, we found an orange thrown against the kitchen ceiling with such ferocity that part of the peel had stuck. My mother immediately went to check on Tommy. I banged on Jack's door, but he wouldn't answer me. I knew he was in there. Light was leaking out of a new hole through the baseboard in the shape of my father's foot. After awhile, I gave up and went to bed. Around midnight, my mother came in and curled up beside me.

———†———

I didn't bank entirely on my mother's hopes for Hawaii. I had fantasies of my own. Say my father was late driving home from work one night and it started raining. The freeways were still new then, vast eight-lane pretzel loops circling the city. The first drops hit the blacktop and all the grease floats up, spangling the tar green, turning the asphalt into Teflon. I watched the evening news. I knew it was the rainy season. I saw footage of cars swerve, skid, pile up, and burst into flames.

My mother stood beside me at the window, absently chewing on a ragged fingernail, staring out at the wet, moonless night. I didn't even have to catch her eye. I knew what she was dreaming because I was dreaming it, too. The sudden knock. The stoic policeman at our front door, holding his dripping hat in his hands, unable to look us in the face.

When my father finally pulled into the garage, looking absurdly vulnerable in his soaking Chevy, in his sodden shoes, I was left with the awful aftertaste of my fantasies.

Later, though, in sleep, my fantasies continued uncensored, blazing with hallucinatory light.

After the rains hit that year, a heat spell began that buckled the driveway and caused the roof to tick and groan. Water was rationed and the topsoil around my father's roses turned as hard as linoleum. By late October, when the Santa Ana kicked in, the ground was so parched, dust devils twisted across the valley. One Saturday, Jack got caught in one. He was walking past a vacant lot when a whirlwind, shaped like a gray brain, rolled over him. His throat tightened, his eyeballs stung, his windpipe clogged up with histamines. By the time he stumbled through the front door, his face looked swollen shut.

I ran to get my father. He was watering what was left of his roses. I dragged him inside by his shirt-sleeve.

Hunkered on the foyer tiles, Jack was clutching his ribs, shrill whistles of air eking out of his small chest.

For a couple of seconds, my father didn't react. He just froze in a crystal of inertia. I barely breathed myself, scared to siphon off any extra oxygen. When I saw Dad wasn't moving, I raced into the kitchen and dialed my mother at work. I garbled details, begged her to come home, probably made it sound worse than it was. When I got back, my father still hadn't moved. His eyes looked red and he was staring at Jack. You could see he wanted to comfort his son, knew something was expected of him, but he didn't know how to begin. Just as some people can't function in a disorderly room, at a sloppy desk, my father couldn't function in the mess of life.

He began to panic. To buy time and get his son breathing again, he turned on the shower, sending a hot deluge onto the tiles. Over the hissing racket, he yelled for me to help Jack into the steam. Even in times of crisis, my father shied away from touching his children.

I half-lugged, half-dragged my brother into the shower, closing the stall doors behind him. To see if he was breathing okay, I cupped my eye to the ribbed glass, but all I could see was my own shallow breath coming in little puffs of panic. Then I saw Jack. He was squatting on the green tiles, his knees up, his swollen head between them—an overinflated red medicine ball topped by a buzz cut. The water darkened his shirt, his pants, his shoes. Steam rose and wafted along the ceiling, dripped from the lightbulb, ran down the wallpaper. My father sat down on the toilet cover, put his head in his hands, and closed his eyes. He said I should take care of things. The dampness touched his caked shoes, unleashing the smell of twigs, leaves, manure, and earth. The window fogged up, blotting out the sun, and, for a moment, it felt as if we were sinking.

When my mother arrived, she took one look at Jack, my immobilized father, the dark wheezing blur of her son. She opened the shower door and scooped up the boy, holding him against her.

Jack's breathing loosened.

"What the hell is wrong with you, Bert? Are you insane? Are you fucking insane?" she said. "I'm taking him to the hospital."

My father started to shake his head. The fear of having reacted badly, of not knowing what was expected of him or how to behave more humanly, was so unnerving to my father that he clung to a more familiar fear, that of spending money.

"You can't do this to me, Lorraine. We can't afford hospitals. Look at him. Look. He's fine. There's no reason to waste the money. Why do you always do this to me?"

In the narrow bathroom, his enormous voice caromed around the walls. My mother lifted Jack to his feet and walked him to the car. I grabbed Tommy and slid in beside her. She gunned the engine. Jack stretched out on the backseat, gulping for air.

Just as we were rolling away, my father ran out onto the driveway, calling us back. He looked stunned that we didn't stop, lost that we'd left him behind. Sometimes I think my father lacked an emotional compass, the mental equivalent of the body's ability to sense, without having to be shown, where the hands are positioned, the feet are set, where the heart resides. He sat down on the curb, squinting into our wake.

The neighborhood whizzed by—a blur of cinder blocks and blue ice plant. I kept my eyes trained on the road, on the gauntlet of stop signs. Only when we neared the hospital and I knew Jack would be all right did I have the nerve to look at him. He was sitting up now, his head back, his breathing a little steadier. His face was still puffy, blotchy, almost inhuman. Only his eyes, within swollen slits, gave a clue to his terror.

———†———

My mother said she didn't care if we had to live in a cardboard refrigerator box and eat dog food, she'd had enough of my father and went to see a divorce lawyer. My brothers and I went with her, waiting out the appointment on a grassy smudge near the office building's doors. After awhile, she came out in tears, her face a rainbow of runny makeup. She said the lawyer had thrown some pretty blunt questions at her. Would my father really pay child support, let alone alimony? Did she have an iota of savings? Any job prospects other than salesgal? Who would take care of us kids while she worked?

The usual blah-blah-blah of adult wariness as far as I was concerned.

On the way home, she and Jack went over our potential budget, our long-shot possibilities, and for a while, things sounded hopeful. (Behind the wheel, her sandal-shod foot gunning the accelerator, my mother was always at her bravest.) She figured she had as much money saved now as she ever would, and after it ran out, who could say? Maybe she'd meet a millionaire. Or we'd find oil in the backyard, move to Brentwood or Bel Air, get in on the real estate boom.

At an interminably long stoplight, she suddenly slumped her forehead against the steering wheel. She said she didn't know how to make a mortgage payment, or buy car insurance, or pay an electric bill. And who would change the lightbulbs? What if they kept fizzling out and she couldn't reach the sockets and the house grew dark? Of all the challenges facing my mother—zilch money, three kids to support—changing the lightbulbs struck her as the most insurmountable.

Over the next couple of weeks, whenever she wasn't working, I found her pacing the kitchen floor, or transfixed by the window, or scrutinizing the want ads, a ravenously chewed pencil clenched between her teeth.

Sometimes she'd crawl into my bed and we'd talk about her fears—loneliness, never being touched again, forgetting to buy lightbulbs, not being able to make it out there—in more detail than I wanted to know. Burrowing my face into the folds of her robe, I could see her worries as transparent threads drifting across the night.

One afternoon, I found her crying in the backyard.

"For God's sake," I said, "*I'll* change the frigging light-bulbs."

"I'm pregnant."

I stared at her.

"Obviously it was an accident, Jill. A stupid, stupid, *stupid* mistake!"

Not being old enough to grasp the idea of loveless sex, I couldn't fathom how she'd been so reckless. One of her night-gowns was torn in the front, and for a moment I thought she might have accidentally touched him during sleep, rolled up against him because of the slope of their bed.

"Oh, God, Jill, I'm stuck! We're stuck. Stuck with your father." She started to pace the length and breadth of the crab-grass. "Unless, of course, I can find someone to give me an abortion."

Her plan was insane: She and I would drive to Tijuana,

cruise the streets until we found a doctor or a clinic or someone to help us. Maybe we'd take the boys along and head south
from there. Up and disappear. If I wanted to help out, I could
learn enough Spanish to translate.

Her scheme was just juvenile enough for me to put stock
in it. Hawaii or Mexico, it really didn't matter to me—I
wanted us out of the valley and free of my father. Besides, I saw
myself in a poncho, donning huaraches, carrying a coconut instead of a thermos to school.

Next day, I approached Rosa, one of the Mexican girls in
my gym class, and asked her to help me translate some phrases
I figured might come in handy. She wrote them down pho-
netically and showed me how to roll my r's.

That afternoon, sitting in an empty parking lot, feeling the
tip of my tongue trip along the roof of my mouth, I practiced
those phrases as I had never practiced anything before.

Is there a clinic nearby?
¿Hay una clinica derce de aquí?

Can you help us?
¿Puedes ayudarnos?

Is there anyone out there who can help us?
¿Hay alguién que nos pueda ayudar?

Which direction should we head in?
¿En cual direccion debemos ir?

Where are we?
¿Adonde estamos?

When I got home, our front door was ajar.

"*¡Hola!*" I shouted.

Nothing.

"*¿Qué pasa?*"

With rush hour gearing up, I couldn't exactly hear the swamp cooler, but I could feel it. Its tremors shimmied through my sandaled feet. I padded into the den.

My mother was crying on the sofa. She knew I was standing there, but she didn't look at me. Her hair, thrashing in the cooler's wind, whipped and slapped against the Naugahyde.

I sat down beside her. She started to say something, shook her head, turned to the bolsters.

I put my arms around her and held her tightly, partly to comfort her, partly not to slip off the cushions, partly to anchor myself to someone.

There was no point in our talking. It was apparent to both of us we weren't going anywhere.

That weekend, I met the Kerkorian sisters at our hide-out—a vacant lot clotted with quack grass, junked sofas, and tires. It was near dusk and the sun had dropped behind the mountains, sending a colossal shadow rolling across the valley. Come nightfall, Julie and Nancy were going to bicycle over to the Fines' house, break in, and steal an ashtray or a candlestick or some silver knick-knack. If they got lucky, Julie bragged, they might stick around long enough to polish off any ice cream in the freezer.

The Fines were off on a family vacation to a dude ranch in Big Timber, Montana. Mr. Kerkorian worked for Mr. Fine, so they had the scoop.

I asked if I could go, too, and rode on the back of Julie's bike, watching our subdivision float by—banks of bright casement windows, sulfur green streetlamps, plaster lawn deers with glass eyes. The sky was dark violet, shot with the pink loopy trails of Lockheed test rockets. Power lines crackled overhead. Opening my mouth, I could feel the wind in my lungs, on my neck, through my beehive.

At the foot of the hills, we jumped off the bikes and trudged up. The houses were bigger here, the grass clipped and manicured. Even the stenciled addresses on the curbs seemed crisper.

Julie used a brick to smash in the Fines' kitchen window. Being the scrawniest, I squeezed between the glass stalactites and unlatched the door. For a couple of minutes, we huddled together on the gray linoleum, waiting for the crack of glass to stop reverberating in our ears. Shafts of streetlights crisscrossed the floor. The oven clock ticked loudly. Keeping low, we tiptoed through the Dutch doors. The Fines had left a lamp burning for security, so we sidestepped its bright halo and started down the hall, opening doors as we went. The master bedroom was wall-to-wall mirrors, the den a jumble of Naugahyde and oak, the daughter's room all pink-and-white flounce.

We stopped and blinked into the pinkness. Normally, one of us would have rolled our eyes and pretended to gag at such daddy-girl froufrou—the canopied bed, its collection of stuffed animals—but we were impressed, mighty impressed. To break the maudlin spell of envy and make Julie and Nancy laugh, I hopped on the bed and bounced up and down.

The canopy creaked.

Julie and Nancy giggled nervously.

I groped for a loose corner of pink wallpaper and yanked off a piece.

Julie and Nancy glanced at each other.

I peeled off some more and waved it above my head like a football pennant.

Then, unable to stop myself, I picked up a cushion with a picture of San Simeon stitched across it and tried to rip it in two. I didn't touch the stuffed animals. I couldn't bear to: I worshiped animals, even pillowed replicas of animals. Instead, I mashed a couple of plastic dolls underfoot.

Next, I started in on the living room. I pulled as many buttons as I could off the recliner chair. I stabbed a letter opener through the flowered sofa. I tramped into the kitchen and unplugged the fridge so all the food would go bad. I scratched FUCK YOU on the stove's surface with fork prongs.

Julie and Nancy hung back in the shadows, watching me with looks of bewildered terror that I mistook for respect.

I grabbed a carton of Neapolitan ice cream out of the now-dead freezer, scooped out three bowlfuls, and sat the Kerkorian sisters down at the breakfast nook. Then, straddling the chair across from them, I ate a little more than my fair share of the chocolate, and when that was gone I greedily licked the spoon.

My mother spent the first months of her pregnancy in stunned sadness. She quit her job as soon as she started to show. Said what was the point of working any longer. Said our escape plans were kaput, that we were stuck with my father forever now. He was furious with her for getting pregnant.

By August, hot, huge, and immobilized, she sat in front of the swamp cooler, watching Watts burn on TV. It was 1966, the second summer of rioting. Cars were torched. Bricks hurtled through smoky space. Store glass shattered into torrents of diamonds. Looters carried away their prizes like game-show contestants. She understood their frustration. Said if she wasn't white and pregnant, she'd go down there and get herself a nineteen-inch color TV and an air conditioner.

My brother was born September 3.

When she phoned me from the hospital, she said Pete was the most beautiful baby she'd ever seen, that he had dimples like Clark Gable.

He didn't look that beautiful to me, but I was crazy about him anyway, charmed by his helplessness and by the way he made my mother's mood spike again.

When she brought him home, I couldn't stop touching him, watching him, monitoring his teeny breath with my own panting awe. Jack and Tommy were just as transfixed. Even my dad seemed beguiled by his new son. But he never held or fed him, and when Pete started to wail, my father wailed even louder, shouting for my mother to take care of *her* kid, to do something around here besides spend his money.

As soon as she felt Pete was up to it, she hankered to get out of the stifling house, hit the road, even if it meant driving in circles. Saturdays, to escape my father's ever-increasing rages, his nonstop bellowing, she strapped Pete in the backseat of the Chevy and cruised the hills. She invited us kids to go with her, but Jack usually declined. Aimless driving seemed pointless to him—but not to Tommy and me. He slid in beside Pete while I rode shotgun. The hills were the posh part of the valley. From up there, gazing down at our neighborhood, the stucco fourplexes, dinky tract homes and truck routes vanished under woolly smog.

Mostly, we meandered, ticking off the weekend hours by our odometer. If our gas ran low and we didn't want my father finding any extra Exxon bills, we killed time by visiting new housing tracts. In the hills, they were called "communities." Buena Vista Community. Hillcrest Community. Encino Estates.

Usually only the model homes were finished—pristine variations on the Spanish hacienda, the English manor, the western ranch house. Behind their squeegee-clean picture windows, the interiors brimmed with glitzy knickknacks and mirrors.

Just as some women might try on expensive dresses to see themselves anew, my mother and I tried on model houses hoping to glimpse ourselves donning another life.

We wandered their rooms for hours, opening closets, sitting on velveteen sofas. If my mother felt risky, she flirted with handsome salesmen, who flirted back.

"What say, ladies? Let me guess. Sisters?"

She pretended it was all a lark, but when we had to go home, I could see a bitter sadness in the frozen shadow of her pause.

One Saturday, coming over the crest of a hill, we stumbled on an enclave of affordability in all that wealth. A group of real estate speculators had bought a canyon, gutted it of chaparral, terraced it with landfill (a euphemism for compressed garbage), and packed it with so many stucco houses that they could be sold at discounts.

The air smelled of plaster and shaved wood and something dank and nameless. The model homes were a lot tinier than we were used to (Woolworth versions of Spanish haciendas), but they still had the same ritzy details Mom, Tommy, and I so admired in the bigger estates—fake gold faucets, shell-shaped bathroom sinks, wall-to-wall mirrors tinted with antique Applikays.

Even at a discount, these houses were priced beyond our reach, but the down payments were low enough—just a shave or two above what we could afford—to lure us back the following Saturday.

A salesman who recognized us and claimed he sympathized with our plight led us to a plot in the bowl of a gully and showed us an unfinished house he thought we might be able to swing.

It was set back from the road and its long, narrow driveway dipped and bowed.

He said it was natural settlement.

The front door stuck when he tried to open it.

He said even houses had to find their sea legs.

The foyer slanted to the left; the bedrooms were small; the back slope had no drainage: Still, my mother wanted it—she wanted it with the same desperate urgency that I had wanted a bubble hairpiece. You see, Mom and I both subscribed to the American belief that through ownership came instant transformation—in my case, from ugly to pretty; in hers, from unhappy to happy.

From that point on, she didn't stop badgering my father about moving. Our house was too small with the new baby. A place in the hills was a terrific investment. Every one of his stock ventures had plummeted, a fact that tormented my father. Why not try real estate? People say location is everything. Besides, Jack and I would start dating soon. We needed to be with our own kind. We needed to date Jewish kids. (The list of home buyers had been filled with Finegolds and Silversteins, and, as the kids in my old school used to say, "You can always count on a kike to have gold and silver in their names.")

I don't recall which one of her arguments worked (although I gravely doubt it was my coming out as a Jewish debutante), but sometime that winter, she broke my father down and we packed up and moved to the sinking house in the hills.

At first, it looked as if my mother had been prophetic: The family was—if not exactly happy—less tense. My father had the project of our unlandscaped backyard (most of which ran perpendicularly up a mountain and had to be planted before the first rains, lest it slide down on us). Digging and grading for hours on end, he channeled all his frustrations into the soil. Jack was no longer tormented at school for his white socks or brains. He even found others of his ilk—pale, pimply boys who carried slide rules in their back pockets instead of combs. Tommy had space to roam in. But it was hopeless for me. With my ratted hair, cracked vinyl miniskirt, and nacreous white lipstick, I had little in common with cardigan-donning classmates who'd just had bas mitzvahs.

Never an attentive student, I found the new courses bewildering, the sense of school spirit strange and repugnant. Just to get by, I took classes like Beginning Business Machines instead of Algebra I. Every morning, half asleep, I'd listen to Mr. Green try to explain the importance of an adding machine to us gum-popping ninth-grade washouts.

"The adding machine is a symbol, a symbol of how you people pull yourselves up by the bootstraps. By the bootstraps. And it's also a metaphor for survival—life goes up and down, and so do adding machines. That's why we're here. Write that down."

No one bothered. He'd given the same lecture last week. I glanced at the clock. Only a minute had dripped by.

"Now take this down. I've seen plenty. Plenty in my fifty-odd years. I was a navy purser in England during World War Two. It's an important job and don't you forget it. Don't you forget it. I had to make a payroll every week and the Brits don't count their pennies. They weigh them. That's why it's called the British pound. Get it? The pound. Some pennies have dirt on them and weigh more; some pennies are worn away and weigh less. Any screwups in the payroll and it had to come out of my paycheck! My paycheck! You better believe I was quaking in my boots when the bank teller poured out those pennies."

On and on he'd ramble until I was overcome with such profound boredom that I'd close my eyes only to see pennies—pennies with dirt on them, soiled pennies, pennies made heavy by the oily touch of human hands.

I wanted to ingratiate myself with the brighter kids, but I didn't know how. They usually ate lunch in tight cliques on the "quad," a dry, bristly lawn that made my legs itch. If it was hot, the girls slipped off their cashmere cardigans and tied them around their necks. They wore gold charm bracelets (as opposed to my clattering slave chains) and had their hair straightened "professionally."

One of the few "quad" girls who sought me out was Rachel Zimmerman. She was shy and plump and laughed at my lewd jokes in art class (the only subject at which I excelled). Both her parents were psychiatrists and she admired the fact that I had a "healthy disregard for authority" and a "rebellious ego." I admired the fact that she had a big suburban house, a pink bedroom set, a swimming pool, a shaggy dog, and money. When she invited me over to dinner, I readily accepted.

I hadn't eaten a real sit-down family meal since we'd left Montreal two and a half years ago. My mother usually served us before my father came home, on paper plates that could be whisked away. If we didn't eat with him, there was less chance of a fight. But there was another reason, too. My father had no table manners. He yelled with his mouth full of peas and forgot to wipe his lips. He pounded the table with his fists until our cutlery rattled and hopped. Sometimes, if we were still eating when he came home, he walked around the table, helping himself to whatever he wanted on our plates—a last french fry, a horded piece of pie. I didn't exactly have time to pick up the finer points of etiquette.

When I sat down with Rachel's family, facing an array of sterling silver forks and spoons, I was convinced her psychiatrist parents could see me for what I was—my father's daughter. I watched Rachel carefully, aped whatever she did. Only once did I slip up and lay my gravy-laden knife onto the table. It left a greasy effigy of itself on the white linen.

Between bites of glazed ham, Mr. and Mrs. Zimmerman politely asked me what I wanted to be (an artist) and which classes I enjoyed most at school (I said I guessed art). When that failed to impress them, I told them I also liked Beginning Business Machines.

Then Rachel's little brother reached for the condiment tray, and a dry piece of mustard as weightless as lint, flecked off his knife and grazed Rachel's hand.

She stopped eating and stared down at it. At school, I'd heard she had a phobia about certain foods—anything yellow or sticky—but I wasn't sure what that meant.

Her mother sighed deeply. Her father picked at his plate with its meticulous array of carved radishes.

"Mom, please get it off me," Rachel said quietly. She was holding her wrist as if her hand belonged to someone else, as if the hand had just slithered up through the floorboards.

"You have a napkin, dear."

"Get it off me! Get it off me now!"

"Can't you get her a wet towel?" Mr. Zimmerman said.

"I will not indulge her like this."

"Just wipe it off her, for God's sake!"

Mrs. Zimmerman threw down her napkin, grabbed a paper towel, and furiously wiped Rachel's hand. Then they all resumed eating, as if nothing had happened. They even made small talk about the neighborhood, unleashed mongrels, and bake sales. By the time Mr. Zimmerman drove me home, I was so bewildered, so disappointed with my glimpse into the good life, I forgot to say my rehearsed "Thank you for having me to dinner, sir, and please tell Mrs. Zimmerman she's a great cook."

Our house was dark. Everyone was asleep save Dad. Despite the late hour, he was hoeing in the yard, a flashlight clamped under his arm. For the last couple of weeks, he'd been gardening three, four hours a night and nonstop on the weekends. I stood by the screen door and watched him. Because of the angle of his flashlight, he worked in a puddle of luminosity. Each time he swung, the beam swept over his shoes, the thwacking blade, his caked shoes again. In the farthest reaches of the light, I could see mud flying out behind him. It flew at frenetic speed, like stones spewing out from under a trapped, whirring tire.

I went inside, curled up on the sofa, and watched TV with the volume low. I didn't care what was on. I just needed the lulling drone, the calming blue light.

———†———

My grades began toppling. I was barely a *C* student, so they didn't have that far to slide, but I managed to bump them all the way down to *D*'s. Worse, I alienated the few teachers I admired. I rarely attended class and when I did, I sauntered in late, brandishing excuse notes I'd obviously penned to get a hoot out of the hoods in the back row. "Jill was unable to attend English yesterday because of terminal acne," or "Jill must be excused from PE for the second time this month because of menstrual cramps."

My mother saw me free-falling. Knowing I loved art and because my father wouldn't let her buy wallpaper, she commissioned me to do a mural in Tommy and Pete's room. We'd just seen *Lust for Life* on the Million Dollar Movie and I felt inspired. Even though van Gogh seemed like a washout, a wild man, a guy who couldn't even remember to comb his hair, he appeared that way only because he harbored a secret inner genius.

I wanted to believe that I possessed an inner genius, too— some glitch in my cells that rendered me special. As a child, I'd displayed an uncanny gift for drawing. With a box of colored crayons, I could re-create my world not only with optical precision but also with waxy ardor. I'd dumped the gift when we'd moved to California, thinking it didn't jibe with my new tough image. When I saw I could have both, I applied myself to the mural as I hadn't applied myself to anything in years. I made dozens of sketches, and when they failed to inspire, I tore them into two, four, eight, sixteen, thirty-two, sixty-four pieces and began again. I swapped rooms with my little brothers so I could work nights as well as weekends. I mulled over my imagery (a primary-colored jungle scene in which all the brightly hued animals hunted one another) to the point where it leaked into my sleep. If I dared walk in a dream, I stepped on a tenuous landscape of my own making. Within no time, I remembered the other reason I'd quit making art. Once I started a project, I became obsessed, even to the point where I scared myself. Sometimes I'd be up for hours, fixated on a square inch of mural (say I couldn't get a tiger's pounce just right) until the paint, fur, teeth blurred, blotting out light and reason. Other times, sure my childhood gift had abandoned me, I'd curl up on the rug, in the cage of shadows cast by Pete's crib.

One night, unable to concentrate because of my father's noisy, ceaseless gardening, I was about to slam the window shut when I caught myself. Stooped over his rosebushes, he looked even more crazed than I. His flashlight was on (it burned every night now, part of his efforts to save money on electricity) and he was digging with quick, jerky stabs. Even in this poor light, I could see he was exhausted. Beside his feet lay a half dozen rosebushes still to be planted, and it was already past midnight.

For a moment, I was tempted to call out to him—not that I knew what I'd say (my father and I seldom spoke). No, I just wanted to divert him from his unrelenting focus and beg him to rest.

Instead, I quietly shut the window. It didn't even make a whoosh in the night.

———†———

A week later, my father's father died. I was putting the last touches on my mural when my uncle called to tell us. It was the first time I'd ever seen my dad on the phone. He stood slumped against the kitchen wall, holding his forehead in his muddy hands. The receiver sat squashed against his ear. I only glimpsed his profile, but it looked blanched and drawn, as if his enormous cheeks had suddenly taken on an insuperable weight. My mother helped him pack (two blue rayon suits bought on sale at Sears) and we drove him to the airport.

On the way home, she wondered out loud if it was in poor taste to play the radio. She said she liked my grandfather and everything, but, after all, he was dead.

Jack said it was okay with him.

Tommy and I said we couldn't even remember the guy.

She spun the dial (all my father's stations were set at stock reports) to something catchy and electric. She turned up the volume and 'drummed her ravenously chewed fingernails against the plastic steering wheel. She tried to sustain a modicum of sadness, but with my father gone and the wind thrashing her hair, you could see how giddy she was.

"In the Jewish tradition, they bury the dead right away, while they're practically still breathing," she said. "But a son has to sit shivah and that takes at least a week, maybe longer." She glanced in the rearview mirror. "Jack, do you remember from your bar mitzvah class how long it takes?"

"We didn't cover shivahs."

"And then there're bound to be papers he has to sort through and that kills time. I mean, he can't work on them while he's mourning. Even your father's not that boorish. You guys think there'll be lots of papers, don't you?"

I said there usually were in the movies.

She stopped at a grocery store and tossed into her basket, along with the usual milk and eggs, a half dozen gourmet foods forbidden under my father's reign——a jar of artichoke hearts soaked in peppered oil, a bunch of pink champagne grapes, one king-size jar of macadamia nuts, and a sirloin steak thicker than a dictionary.

That night we ate——no, we gorged ourselves in front of the TV. When Jack plopped down on the sofa with a third helping, I noticed he'd accidentally left the kitchen lights on. Sighing loudly, he started to shamble back.

My mother grabbed his wrist. "Let them burn," she said.

Then I reached over and cranked up the switch on the pogo-stick pole lamps (normally, my father made us sit in dingy remoteness). The lamps shot three halos of glare onto the TV screen; they practically blanched out the picture.

No one bothered to adjust them.

A couple of minutes later, my mother stood up, stretched, handed Pete to me, then drifted into the bathroom, the hall, the foyer, leaving incandescence in her wake.

By the time we went to bed, our house was ablaze, burning up watts like kindling. Just to be able to sleep, we had to shut our bedroom doors to the brilliance. But some of it leaked in. An uncanny light. Like the hallucinatory glow of Las Vegas at midnight, or the hypnotic afterimage of a flashbulb, or the unearthly light the dead are said to be greeted with in the next world.

————†————

When my father came home, he didn't say anything about the funeral, or his mother's emotional state, or even how Montreal had changed.

I didn't trust his silent grief, but then again, I'd never grieved. The only mourning I'd seen was at the movies—all howling and Technicolor tears. My father's numbness fooled me—it would take the death of a lover, a half dozen friends, and my own father before I'd feel that very numbness myself—and I watched him with suspicion, even contempt. Sometimes I think that compassion is not innate to the heart, that it has to enter us with each childhood scrape and hurt, like tiny bacteria.

My father mourned in his own way and when his grief finally passed, terror replaced it—a terror so black, it made all his other fears seem like feeble preliminaries.

Any hour of the day, you might find him immobilized on the sofa, like something someone had carved, or pacing the yard in his bathrobe, breathless with anxiety, a tiny blue vein jumping on his temple.

It's hard to say why he was so frightened: His stocks had gone down; without his father, he felt there was no one to catch his fall; or maybe the house was just costing more than he bargained for.

One of my brothers once said that whatever you experience in the dead of night, at the hour of the wolf, when all your terrors come out and share your bed, is what my father experienced twenty-four hours a day, every day, even in the tender, hopeful light of morning.

I think my father was autistic, that he tied his shoes, mourned his dad, planted his roses in a sealed existence; that his rages and fears bubbled up from his being, hissing and exploding within him like seltzer shaken in an airtight bottle. Even his aversions to bathing or changing his underwear weren't meant to punish anyone. He simply didn't understand what it was to be comfortably human, let alone how to endear himself to another living soul.

That spring, he got crazier and crazier. The volume of his furies cranked up again, but now, with us living in a canyon shaped like the Hollywood Bowl, his bellowing bounced off the rocks, boomed around the landfill.

I could hear him when I got on the school bus in the morning, when I fell asleep at night.

My mother and I tried wandering again, but visiting model homes only depressed us now. Sometimes, just to keep away, we'd park the car on any old street and sit there for what seemed like hours, staring, heat-baked, sipping tepid colas out of collapsing straws.

Nights, the instant he came home, he'd scrutinize us the way a drill sergeant eyeballs a barracks of green recruits. I think he wanted to find something wrong. Say there was no fresh fruit in the house. He'd stand before the open fridge, blanched by its glacial light, and stare at—no, fixate on—the plastic bin where fruit should have been.

"Okay, what happened to my peaches? What happened to the goddamn peaches? This is my house. My house. There should be peaches waiting for me when I get home. Sure, sure, the kids ate the peaches. Lord high-and-mighty Jack does nothing around here, doesn't do a goddamn thing to help his father, but he eats his father's peaches. Does she care? Noooooo. She probably encourages the kids. She probably hides peaches all over their goddamn rooms. Why the hell can't there be peaches?"

On and on it went, until the taste of peaches soured for me permanently.

Weekends, from dawn to dusk, he demanded Jack work in the garden with him, side by side, like Chinese peasants, farmer and mule, ox and ox. The heat was insufferable. He allowed no breaks save a quick lunch. His landscaping projects had grown insane. Hand-dug trenches for miles of sprinklers. Hand-dug ponds for fish. A slipping mountain that should have been held back by bulldozers was picked away at by axes and shovels.

Around three, Jack inevitably rebelled and they went at each other with shouts and shoves, dirt clods and threats. If my mother was home, she'd charge out the screen door to shield her son. (You could see the door shiver in her wake.) If she was out, I'd take her place, easily staving off my father with the soft end of a broom. He wasn't a particularly violent man; he never swung back at me. Mostly, he slumped against the stucco wall and asked why his children hated him.

Saturday evenings, if he hadn't hidden the distributor cap, my mother drove us to the local cinema. It was before ratings, and she let us see everything—*Valley of the Dolls, Ship of Fools, Who's Afraid of Virginia Woolf?* In the smoky blackness, on the fake velveteen seats, the hypnotic cone of light spilling across the screen, I'd sit alone and practice necking with my cold, oblivious wrist, kissing it with the same passion that Oskar Werner applied to Simone Signoret's arched throat, desperate to savor what the taste of love might be like.

On the way home, my mother usually drove at an imperceptible crawl, lurching to dead stops at dead intersections. By the way she furiously wiped her nose, I knew she was crying. Sometimes, without our even discussing it, she'd idle the car at the hem of our driveway and wait for him to go to bed.

One night, unable to take it any longer, she woke my father up and told him to leave. A couple of minutes later, she came into my room, shaking as if someone had drenched her with ice water. She said he wouldn't listen to her. She said he'd covered his ears with his hands and turned away, feigning snores and oblivion.

Next morning, he pretended not to have heard her. But I noticed the change. Whenever we passed him in the hall, he refused to look at us. When a dish dropped, a roast burned, a bulb blew, he barely even screamed at us. You could see him shutting down.

Mostly, we sat at one end of the house, he at the other. Immobile, shrouded in blue smoke, a mottled cigar leaf hanging from his open lips, he watched TV westerns all night long—*Maverick, Have Gun Will Travel, Wagon Train, Bonanza.* Or he would garden. At this point, I know he was still gardening obsessively, eighteen, sometimes twenty hours at a stretch. And I'm confused. Everything's jumbled up. I see him out there (sweating, panicked), hoeing to the theme song of *Bonanza,* to the thunder of horse hooves, the crackle of fire, the map of home burning, burning.

Then the thudding in my ears ceases; it's no longer horse hooves, but only my own pulse banging.

He sets aside his hoe and squints into the darkness. It must be dark. A reading lamp burns somewhere in the house. Its circle of light, as fleeting as a smoke ring, floats toward him. If he peeked through the window, he'd see his children sleeping, but he doesn't peek through the window. Instead, he picks up a shovel, jabs it into the earth, and begins digging a sprinkler trough he will never finish.

———†———

The rains came—twenty-eight days without end. Doors swelled shut. Carpets grew spongy. Wallpaper warped, then peeled. On TV, my brothers and I watched a bluff split and crumble, a dam crack, a canyon fill up like a bathtub. And the cantilevered houses, the ones built precariously over cliffs, fell in avalanches of crystal and sodden rosewood, marble and broken glass.

Our own tenuous landfill and all it was built upon—silt, sand, compressed garbage, balls of aluminum foil—began to sag.

For twenty-eight days, my father waded through gigantic waves of rain and sleet, trying to sandbag the slippage, unclog the cement pipes. One by one, his rosebushes washed away, his trenches collapsed, his fish ponds turned thick and swampy.

Huddled together on the living room sofa, my mother, brothers, and I watched him through the glass doors as he tried to hold back the mountain, stop the mud, rocks, and sludge from razing his garden, upending our house.

We never offered to help.

Ten times a day, Jack was dragged out by his collar, only to sneak back inside. My mother and I hid him in closets, then returned to the sofa, to our "box seats" at this private deluge.

I think we wanted our house to go. I know we wanted our world to slide away.

Now and again, an enormous rainbow appeared through a tear in the clouds, bouncing its spectrum off anything wet—a glistening boulder, a glassy puddle. Beside my mud-splattered father, the pomp and splendor left me unspeakably sad. I could never have put it in so many words, but for the first time in my life, I sensed that nature's beauty was merciless.

———†———

"I want you to move out," my mother told him. "Now, Bert. This weekend. Please, I can't take it any longer."

It was the first Saturday after the rains had stopped. She was standing in the dark hall, talking to his back. My father, without turning around, gave a stiff shake of his head, as if to clear it of rainwater, then returned to his ravaged yard, to his ceaseless digging.

I wandered over to the window and watched him—a blur of muscle, shovel, panic, and mud. After awhile, he tramped back inside and looked for my mom.

She was in the bath, door locked, a racket of water pounding the tub. Pressing his brow against the jamb, he began stammering, words blurring into one another.

The water quit. "Find an apartment, Herbert. Please, just find an apartment."

That night, my mother slept on the sofa. When I got up for a glass of water, I saw him standing near her, staring intently. Street light eked in through the drapes, penciling the room yellow. Leaning over her, my father's face seemed so pale, it looked like the stab of an afterimage.

Next morning, he still wouldn't leave. Jack spoke to him. My mother pleaded with him. I dragged over the *Pennysaver* and read him the rental listings. I even offered to go with and help him find an apartment.

Finally, in abject frustration, my mother tried to push him out the door. For a moment, he stared at her retreating figure (a flurry of pink robe vanishing down the dark hall), then followed me to the car.

We drove in silence. We scoured the floor of the valley for red rental signs. We looked at countless efficiency apartments—tiny rooms with squat refrigerators and beds that emerged from walls, from closets, from cabinets, from sofas, once from an overstuffed reclining chair. If the units had a stove, they were called "singles'." If all that heated up was a hot plate, they were called "bachelors'." Some places had small kidney-shaped pools in their cement courtyards. These lent the apartments a kind of glint and glimmer, and, despite the extra cost, I urged my father to consider them.

At the Montego Arms (all the buildings had names—the Palms, Casa de Lujo, Country Manor), I sat on an orange sofa while my father stared out the casement window. It was our second visit. I thought it was the best of the lot. Pool reflections swam along the walls. The ceiling was made out of stucco and glass flecks. Near the numbered car slots sat a couple of empty planters I figured he might be able to grow roses in.

Rubbing his eyes as if he had sand in them, he sat down beside me (I could feel the crunch of bedsprings) and asked if this was just a bad dream.

I wanted to answer him, comfort him, but since we rarely spoke, let alone said anything personal, I was struck dumb.

After a while, to relieve the awful silence, I suggested we test the sofa bed to see if the mattress was firm enough. We tossed aside the cushions, yanked out the frame, and wordlessly lay down, side by side, on the striped mattress, in the stippled sunlight.

That night, I helped him pack, folding his blue suits, his polyester shirts, his stiff gardening clothes. Now and again, rummaging through a drawer in search of a missing sock, he'd grab the one that was left, as if seizing proof of my mother's inconsiderateness, and scream for her. We thought it was best that she stay away. When he couldn't find his checkbook, he yanked out a drawer and tossed its contents across the room. I dodged a whirlwind of pencils, boxer shorts, hankies, and pens.

Around midnight, I snuck off to bed. Twice I awoke to the

sound of murmuring. It was my mother assuring him that she wouldn't change her mind.

In the morning, she locked herself in the bathroom while Jack and I carried his suitcases to the car. When we came back, he still hadn't put on his shoes. He said no one could force him to go, that it was his house, he'd goddamned well paid for it. But his voice sounded flat and when Jack handed him his shoes, he obediently slipped them on.

We walked him to the car, opened his door, and stood with him in awkward silence. The rank smell of dead cigars wafted up from the ashtray. My father made no move to dig out his keys. Not knowing what to do, Jack offered his hand and wished him good luck. I patted his shoulder and said we'd see him soon. We hurried back inside, closed the door, then slumped against it. My mother tiptoed out of the bathroom, motioning us to keep quiet. She gingerly leaned against the drawn drapes, head cocked, listening.

His car sat idle, dead. After a while, she sank down on the cold linoleum, one slippered foot folded under her, and started crying. She said he would never leave.

Tommy and Pete wandered in, curious to see what was going on, and she practically batted them back into their room.

Finally, we heard his car start, saw its phantom shape ripple across the drapes and vanish.

Next morning, however, he was parked at the bottom of our driveway. I had to wave to him as I trudged to school, nod at him as I scuffed home.

My mother refused to leave the house, wouldn't even crack the drapes. For six days, he practically lived out there, holed up in his oven-hot Chevy. Now and again, one of us kids took him apple juice, a hard-boiled egg, a wax-paper column of Ritz crackers.

One afternoon, without telling anyone, I slipped out the back door and hid in a tangle of bushes a half dozen feet from his hood. The sun burned behind me so I was all ghost and glare. The street sat mirrored in his windshield—listing antennae, buckled driveways, aluminum mailboxes. If I kept low and squinted, I could just make out my father's face. His eyes were shut, but I knew he wasn't sleeping. (My father couldn't sleep without a pillow.) No, by the way his lids were clenched, I figured he was obsessing, batting one thought back and forth in his brain. And more than likely, it wasn't about the demise of his marriage. More than likely, it was about Jack and me. (My father always dwelled on his last indignity.) Probably, he was picturing his two oldest children escorting him—no, *dragging* him—out of *his* house and into the car. Probably, he was playing this image over and over again—never varying it, never allowing it to accumulate meaning—so that, even though Jack and I only walked him ten feet to the Chevy, in his mind, we had dragged him halfway around the world.

I sat down on a rock, drew up my knees, and wrapped my arms around them. His brows were still bunched, his eyes slammed shut. And as the suburban sights imploded on his windshield, I knew he hadn't the slightest inkling of why he had been banished.

Next morning, my father finally drove off. My mother was—to put it mildly—deliriously relieved. Even my brothers caught her mood. But not me. Having been to my father's apartment, having chosen it for him, I could picture his new life—I couldn't stop picturing it.

I saw him unlock his iron-hot doorknob, saw the pea green walls, orange sofa bed, and squat fridge. Cigarette burns speckled the carpet and a rust stain, shaped like a dog's bone, lay under the sink.

Knowing the full force of my father's fury, I saw him throw down his two suitcases and yank out the sofa bed—a geological eruption of cushions, steel, springs, and mattress. Since Dad would never deign to make a bed, I imagined him lying down on the bare, disheveled surface to watch the daylight slide across the walls and fade. I knew he was lonely and terrified. By dark, I pictured him curled—no, balled up—under the pool reflections. They swam over the ceiling, hit the zillions of glass flecks in the stucco and sparkled. He appeared to be dreaming under an unknown firmament, or perhaps just our galaxy seen from the other side.

PART

----+----

TWO

The family's center was gone. As crazy as my father had been, he was the focal point around and against which we had always rallied.

My brothers and I felt numb, heady, dazed. Even my mother appeared shell-shocked. For the first couple of weeks, her mood vacillated between catatonic stillness and manic freedom. To calm herself down, she redecorated the house. On a minuscule budget (we had no income), she plastered plate-size yellow daisy stickums all over the kitchen walls, ceiling, and cabinets. (My job was to snip the cabinets free when she accidentally stickumed them shut.) She threw out the brown Sears drapes and hung glassy love beads over the windows. Sometimes, while supine on the sofa, watching the beads' reflections (strings of scintillation playing over the stickums), my future seemed bright and limitless. Other times, finding my mother shut up in the bathroom, muting her sobs with the bunched hem of her robe, I'd be overwhelmed by such abject terror, I could almost feel my father's presence.

My mother went to court and was temporarily awarded sixty-nine dollars per child per month. Even by 1967 standards, it was a pittance. Four pairs of sneakers, lunch money, a leaky fridge, and a spiked water bill could drain our income by half. The medical coverage my father paid for (at the court's insistence) had a deductible so immense that it was virtually useless.

When our worldly goods were finally divvied up, my father got the stocks and Chevy, my mother the house (unpaid for) and the station wagon, an enormous winged, rattling brown machine. Mornings, watching her steer it down the narrow driveway to look for work (a trail of oil, like a snail's path, gleaming in her wake), I grew so panicked over the car's failing gaskets and the cost of repairing them, my throat would tighten and my ears pop. Without my wanting to, I'd taken over my father's guard post on worrying.

The first job she landed was for two swarthy, huffy brothers. They ran an import-export business out of their garage and hired my mom to sell a line of Turkish coats. The coats were what the brothers called a "by-product." All rawhide and fleece, the coats were imported to act as a wrapper for the their real product—a smuggled something they kept in the Deepfreeze.

The coats smelled peculiar. On dry days, they gave off a faint goatish musk; on damp days, a pungent barnyard scent. At the first sign of fog, she loaded them into airtight plastic trash bags to minimize the odor.

All summer, six days a week, while Jack and I baby-sat the

boys, my mother wheeled up and down Sunset Strip trying to sell her wares. It was the year of be-ins and people wanted their clothes "natural," albeit not quite so natural as these. If luck held, she sold one or two coats a day. When we heard her car pull into the driveway, we charged out the front door, anxious to see how much she'd made.

There was an illustration called *The Travails of Pioneer Life* in my American history textbook. It showed a knot of scrawny children dashing out of a sod hovel to embrace their long-lost, hide-toting father. Underneath the picture, in tiny, almost indecipherable print, the caption read: "Because of the rough-and-ready life, the pioneer attitude was 'every man for himself; the strong will survive, and the weak will perish.' "

In addition to the coats, my mother sold a line of greeting cards—pink birthday bunnies, purple get-well irises, grinning Grandmother's Day grandmothers—artwork so saccharine, it made Hallmark look saucy. The ditties inside sang of speedy recuperations and ageless birthdays. Whenever she felt lonely, she took me with her to work the dime stores. I learned to take inventory and restock the cards, to cram as many as I could into the stacks. Sometimes while hunkered on my knees, staring up at the bleachers of pastel-colored cards (a Muzak version of "Yesterday" playing in the background), I'd slip under the spell of their sentimentality, turn wistful and sappy, until the ring of the cash register jarred me back. Now and again, my mother sold a new line of, say, sympathy cards and chalked up a bonus.

Obviously, at a ten-buck commission per coat and a nickel a card, these were nowhere jobs. So at night, she studied to be a court stenographer. Sitting between my brothers and me in front of the TV, she batted the keys of her rented stenotype (a minuscule typewriter that stood on a flamingo-thin leg and spewed out a tongue of rolled paper), taking dictation from *McHale's Navy, The Robert Goulet Hour,* reruns of *I Love Lucy.* Around 11:00 P.M., she turned off the TV and, in a false, hearty, officious voice, read the dialogue back to us.

Lucy, what are you doing here?
Hiya, Ricky.
Lucy! I told you you couldn't be in the show. Ai,
    caramba!
Now, Ricky.
Lucy, what do you have to say for yourself?
Aw, Ricky, I love you.
I love you, too, honey.

Then she slumped her forehead against the keys and shut her eyes.

Sometimes, despite my mother having a queen-size mattress all to herself now, she reverted back to crawling into my bed after the boys fell asleep.

She said she was sorry to wake me but that she was scared, really scared, we might have to go back to my father. Said going back to him would be like burying us all alive. Said she wanted to make a good life for her kids but that no one had taught her any skills to survive. Said I had to prepare myself—we might not be able to make it out there.

66

And I'd try to envision us going back to him. For some reason, my imagined reunions never took place at our house, only at the Montego Arms.

My brothers and I would be standing beside our cardboard suitcases in his sunstruck courtyard. My father would be staring out of his casement window. I was never sure if he saw us—the sun and the smog blanched out everything. Behind the glare of his window, he'd be wearing a look of pained, addled distraction, as though he'd just lost his wallet and was trying to recall where it could be. It was the same look he wore the one and only time he came to see us kids that summer.

———†———

By October, the import-export brothers had vanished. They left a boarded-up garage and a slew of rubber checks. My mother had toted around their cumbersome coats all September for nothing. The greeting-card business, hardly profitable in the best of times, slipped into the doldrums until Christmas. And no matter how hard my mother practiced her court stenography, she couldn't break the two-hundred-word-a-minute barrier—the supposed speed at which witnesses prattle and criminals confess.

One morning, still puffy from sleeplessness, she woke me up and told me to warm up the car. I got dressed, turned over the motor, and fingered the choke. A plume of exhaust chugged out the tailpipe. I eased the accelerator up and down as delicately as one might pump a piano pedal. I was dying to learn how to drive. Then she appeared, toting her purse, and without so much as mentioning where we were going, nudged me aside and took over the wheel.

We drove to the Los Angeles County Department of Welfare and Human Services (which, because of the graffiti and the sign's missing letters, read HUMAN VICES). I didn't want to get out of the car. I said I didn't think we'd sunk this low.

My mother snapped open her purse, clawed through the junk, and chucked her checkbook onto my lap.

"There's nothing in there, Jill. What would you have me do?"

The building's lobby was packed and smoky. Finger marks ringed the elevator buttons and lipstick-stained cigarette butts filled the planters. (The women passing through here wore all shades of lipstick—Lady Pink to Fuchsia Nights.) On the second floor, my mother took a number, then got into a long, noisy queue. I heeled the back wall and pretended to be above it all. I kept glancing at my wrist as if I owned a watch and had somewhere pressing to go.

After a five-hour wait, we were granted a five-minute interview. The social worker, a reed-thin woman in cat glasses, waved my mother over with her emery board.

"Are you a U.S. citizen?" she asked.

"I'm a permanent resident—I have my green card," my mother said.

"Married?"

"Divorced."

"Children?"

"Three boys and a girl."

"Ages?"

"Sixteen, fourteen, eight, and one."

"Employed?"

"No."

"Do you have proof of no employment?"

"I have a stack of bad checks," my mother said. She rummaged through her purse for the import-export brothers' rubber checks, then fanned them out across the social worker's steel desk. (We'd redeposited the checks so many times, they were more stamped than a passport.)

"These are paychecks? You have a job?"

"I *had* a job."

"Any other source of income?"

"Child support."

The social worker scribbled that down.

"Listen," my mother said, "my kids can eat through their allotments in a week."

"Do you reside in an apartment or a house?"

"A house."

"Rent or own?"

"Own. Or at least the bank owns it."

"Do you have a car?"

"Yes."

"Make and year?"

"A 1961 Dodge Dart station wagon."

"Any other capital investments?"

My mother shook her head no.

"I'm sorry. You don't qualify for aid."

"What?"

"You own a house and a car. You have capital investments."

"You're joking? The wagon has over a hundred thousand miles. The house is a white elephant. It sits—no, it floats—on landfill. Next big rain and it's going to wash away."

"I'm sorry, Mrs. Ciment. To qualify for aid, you can't own a house or a car."

"But no one in their right mind would buy them off me. Look, lady, I've got four kids to feed."

"I don't make the rules."

"Isn't there—"

"I don't make the rules."

"But—"

"Mrs. Ciment, the rules are the rules."

My mother gave a deep sigh, then just sat there shaking her head. She wouldn't stop. I nudged her shoulder. I tugged on her sleeve. I scooped the rubber checks off the desk.

"Leave them," my mother said. Rising to her feet, she grabbed her purse and stormed out of the building.

I dogged her to the car.

She drove crazily, gunning the engine, crunching the brakes. She swerved so sharply, she missed the parking lot's exit. We joggled and bounced over the six-inch curb. On the boulevard, she charged into traffic, switched lanes erratically. She blasted her horn at any slight—a dawdling pedestrian, a fast driver. Only near the freeway did she start to slow down (my mother was humbled by freeways) and veered almost gingerly onto the on-ramp. We came to a bumpy halt on the emergency shoulder. Without saying a word, she got out of the car and walked down the gravel bank toward the NO BICYCLES OR PEDESTRIANS PAST THIS POINT sign. A semi thundered by, dusting her with sand in its gusty wake. Her pink kerchief blew off and drifted away like smoke. She closed her eyes and tilted her face toward the sun. Then, blinking rapidly, as if coming out of an ether dream, she turned around and got back into the car. We drove on. I kept my gaze trained out the window, on the rush of tumbleweeds and off-ramps. To end the silence and my furious nail biting, I prattled on about anything and everything—schemes, hairdos, my upcoming learner's permit, my imbecilic teachers, poor grades, and grandiose dreams. I didn't mention the welfare office. No one had to tell me that subject was verboten now.

———†———

One of the divorcées in my mother's stenography class suggested Mom try her hand at market research. The pay was paltry, the woman admitted, but the hours were flexible, and if my mother was clever, she'd eventually learn how to pad her billing hours and up the ante. She gave my mother the phone number of an old widow who ran a small firm in the north valley.

Mrs. McCaffrey, widowed since World War II, had single-handedly raised her own four children and immediately felt a kinship with my mother. She hired her to work the pre-Christmas rush. When Mom hinted that Jack and I were old enough to work after school and weekends, Mrs. McCaffrey signed us on, too.

She was the largest woman I'd ever met. Fat hung from her wrists, accumulated around her ankles. Sometimes, watching her waddle toward us in her billowing pink bougainvillea-print muumuu, it looked as if a waft of California—its flora and hugeness—was coming to save us.

She ran her market-research surveys out of a number of malls scattered along the foothills—the Galleria, El Plaza,

Topanga Plaza, Foothill Mall. We worked Foothill Mall. It was shaped like a barbell, weighted on each end by a department store—May Company (for the workaday gal) and Bullock's (for the ritzier set). In between, pet, brassiere, and potpourri shops eked out a living. We set up near the escalator on what Mrs. McCaffrey called the "gazebo." Although the mall had a futuristic theme (pink and purple neon lights, a Plexiglas fountain), the gazebo was pure nineteenth-century Americana—a white antebellum stage with fluting. In the mall's glory days, it had been used for community events—high school cheerleading displays and Muscular Dystrophy drives. Now it had gum wads stuck under its chipped balustrades.

All day long, the escalator hummed, the fountain babbled, and though it was only mid-November, Christmas music (a different song for every store) drifted across the floor. The big holiday gala, a thirty-foot plastic Christmas tree with glow candles and live carolers stood next to Bullock's. On Saturdays from noon to three and then again from six to nine, the high notes of "Away in a Manger" and "O Little Town of Bethlehem" reached us.

Tinsel and spray-painted snow brimmed in all the display windows.

We were interviewing people about their barbecuing habits. Did they use charcoal or kindling? How many times a week did they grill? Did Mom marinate the steaks? Did Dad rule the coals?

Since I couldn't spell and was grammatically illiterate, my job was to act as a barker and lure in potential respondents. My mother and Jack did the actual interviewing. Mrs. McCaffrey, too old and obese to stand, straddled two steel folding chairs and attended to what she called "mall diplomacy."

Most of the stores wanted us out (they rightly claimed we cut into their customers' shopping time), and Mrs. McCaffrey was constantly having to haggle over where I could stand (ten feet from a shop door) and when I could solicit (not during the noon bustle).

I didn't want to solicit at all. I loathed the servile tone I assumed when I asked strangers to spare me a moment. I cringed when they brushed me off like a beggar and I hated my big salesgal's smile when they didn't. Sometimes, I ambled around the escalator just asking people what time it was. (From Mrs. McCaffrey's vantage point, it looked as if I was still soliciting—a glance at the wristwatch being the universal signal for "I'm busy.") Unfortunately, the ruse only kept me unbearably aware of every hour, half hour, minute, and second that passed.

The closer it got to Christmas, the more distraught I became. I'd just started high school that fall and, although the mall was on the far end of the valley, now and again a bevy of my new classmates showed up to carouse the Bullock's bins. I could have handled their seeing me working in a roller rink or something rebellish like that, but being caught toiling with my family on a gazebo was insufferable to me—it reeked of poverty and immigrantdom.

If Mrs. McCaffrey wasn't looking, I snuck off the second I spied a familiar face. Sometimes my mother fetched me; sometimes she didn't. She was too spent to care. Jack was fed up with my antics: He had to cover for me when I fled. If he wasn't stuck interviewing a respondent, he'd charge up the escalator after me, grab me by my bony wrist, and yank me back.

One Saturday, after I'd wandered away for the umpteenth

time, he told our mother that if I didn't shape up, he'd quit; he was sick to death of working with little Miss High-and-Mighty.

It was near closing time. Mrs. McCaffrey had already left. My mother sat slouched on a folding chair, one stockinged foot up on the chipped railing.

"He's a liar," I said. "I was only taking a chocolate-bar break."

"Yeah, we really believe you, Jill."

"Jack, what do you want from me?" my mother asked.

"Tell her it's not fair."

My mother closed her eyes. "It's not fair," she said.

"Tell her she can't just sashay off when the whim strikes her or when her little uppity friends show up."

"You tell her, Jack. She doesn't listen to me."

"She doesn't listen to anyone; she's completely spoiled," he said. He picked up a stack of questionnaires and began frenetically counting them. "You know, we're not even halfway done with these barbecuing questionnaires. I just want to know—am I supposed to finish them all by myself?"

"Can it, Jack."

"Well, am I?"

"I'm exhausted, Jack. Drop it."

But Jack wouldn't let up. He kept needling my mother until her mercurial temper blew.

She grabbed a handful of surveys and threw them at him. They flew around the gazebo like startled fowl. "Do you think I give a shit about barbecuing! Do you think I give a fuck about marinades? Do you? Just leave me the hell alone. Will you kids please, please, please, *please* just leave me alone." She pressed her fingertips to her temples and paced the gazebo from one antebellum post to another.

I knew that everyone was watching. I stepped backward off the stage and rode the escalator up, into the colored lights, the smell of chocolate, the harmonious chorus of "O little town of Bethlehem, / how still we see thee lie! / Above thy deep and dreamless sleep / the silent stars go by; / yet in thy dark streets shineth / the everlasting Light / the hopes and fears of all the years / are met in thee tonight."

———†———

That evening, after picking up Pete at the baby-sitter's, we drove home in seething silence. Tommy was waiting for us in the dining room, drinking a glass of lemonade. He'd spent the afternoon with my father. (Mom had been begging Dad for months to take Tommy Saturdays so that he wasn't always left to wander the mall unsupervised.) This Chanukah was the first time my father had agreed to it. Tommy was on strict orders from Mom to get Dad to buy him a new pair of shoes for the holidays. Tommy's feet were outgrowing her budget. Instead, Dad had bought him a can of low-cal lemonade. Having just invested in NutraSweet stock, Dad wanted to show Tommy the new sugarless future.

When my mother heard this, she went nuts, smashed a plate, then locked herself in her room with Pete. Jack was already holed up in his. I went into the kitchen and found Tommy crouched at the breakfast table, trying desperately to enjoy the last of Dad's Chanukah lemonade. He was sipping it slowly, as if it was Courvoisier. I grabbed the glass out of his hand and, in front of his smarting eyes, pretended to pour it down the sink.

"Boy," I said, "you sure can be bought cheap."

Then I handed the glass back to him, went into my room, and slammed the door. The bang hardly registered. The other doors in the house had already been slammed shut.

J ust as we fell into a workaday
hopelessness, my mother met
a man. She didn't bring him
around at first, saying she needed the romance of being alone
with him. But I had my suspicions; she didn't want to scare him
off with her brood. His name was Aaron and he'd been a clas-
sical violinist before a car crash shattered his elbow and ended
his career. He now worked in the wholesale meat trade. And
even though I knew he was from Brooklyn, something about
the violin and his tragic accident and the hint of imported
cologne on my mother's clothes made me envision him with a
European accent, sporting a smoking jacket with red velvet
lapels.

Up until Aaron, my mother had been dating traveling salesmen in polyester suits and truckers in cowboy hats. One of her
dates had shown up wearing a silver belt buckle the size of a
lunch plate. It had the lyrics of "Tie a Yellow Ribbon 'Round
the Old Oak Tree" tooled into its border.

She'd met her dates at singles bars—the Fireside Inn,
Thank God It's Friday, and Loopy's. She said all the bars were

the same—garnet red rooms packed with divorcées nursing wine spritzers and raucous Casanovas knocking back scotches. Sometimes, if I was still awake when she came home, she'd fix us a snack, then walk me through the gauntlet of her evening: the jostle of men, her best quips, the plumber—"a cross between an ugly Robert Mitchum and a good-looking Ed Sullivan"—who said he'd memorized all the positions in the *Kama Sutra,* all 2,701.

Saturday nights, before she and I went out carousing (me to the roller rink, she to the bars), we'd stand hip-to-hip before the bathroom mirror, naked, lips pursed, brushing our hair. Without meaning to be cruel, I'd point out the enigmas of her aging, the twenty-two-year differences between our bodies—her crow's-feet, my taut stomach, her mole with its protruding hair, my blond down—and ask if she wanted to be fifteen again.

Without batting a false eyelash, she said, "I'd rather be dead."

One evening, she brought Aaron home with her. He wasn't at all what I'd envisioned. He was squat rather than graceful, bald rather than gray-templed, and had a gruff Brooklynese rather than a suave Viennese accent. But I would have considered him for a stepdad (I was ready to consider just about anyone). He kissed my mother affectionately and tried to take an interest in us kids. But I saw the strain. He wasn't used to the tumult of children, and even though we were on our best behavior, our sheer numbers made us irksome. During dinner, Tommy kept knocking his sneaker against the table leg. Jack cuffed his ear. Pete cried from the constraints of eight hours in nursery school. And I acted so coy and sweet that even

I got nauseous. By ten o'clock, you could see Aaron was antsy to leave.

That Friday night, my mother came home early. She stood outside my door for a moment, then went to bed. Our shared wall was as thin as wax paper. I could hear her crying. She sounded as if she was choking on a tiny fish bone. I went into her room. She lay curled on the sheets, her back to me, her feet drawn up.

I nestled against her and put my arms around her.

She shrugged, then burrowed her face deeper into the pillows. "I feel like such a fool," she said. "I thought he loved me. The prick went back to his old girlfriend."

I lay quietly in the dark. A garbage truck clattered by, followed by the ceaseless barks of a tethered dog.

"There's nothing to say, Jill. Do you hear me? Nothing."

In the morning, her side of the bed was empty. Splotches of mascara lay caked all over her pillow. She was pacing by the window, wearing last night's sleep-crumpled blouse.

"I'm going on a sales trip and I want you to come with me. That is, if you can miss school for a couple of days. You don't have exams or anything, do you?"

I said I couldn't think of a single one.

"Because I just don't want to stick around here, kiddo. I'll go mad."

Next morning, while she gave Jack spending money to take care of Tommy, I strapped Pete in the backseat of the wagon and loaded her stock—a slew of new greeting cards and a tie-dyed T-shirt line she'd recently picked up. (The material was so bright, it looked as if it had been dipped in the chimerical colors of a hallucination.)

She drove in silence.

An hour out and she veered into the emergency lane. She said we were lost. I glanced back. She'd just passed a four-tiered junction of ramps and loops and must have overshot our exit. When I pointed this out, she sighed sarcastically and threatened to drive the four hundred yards backward. Then she closed her eyes and asked if I was hungry.

I shook my head no. We had just eaten breakfast.

"Well, *I'm* starving," she said.

She crawled along the slow lane until she spied a food court—a pseudovillage of upscale eateries, each sporting the decor of its cuisine. The fish restaurant had nets and driftwood, the Mexican one a plaster saguaro.

She pulled off the freeway and into the parking lot but didn't make any move to open her door. The sun was at its zenith. Our seats became searingly hot.

"What are you in the mood to eat?" I asked.

She tilted her forehead against the steering wheel. "You decide," she said softly.

I traipsed past the restaurants, squinting at the posted menus. I was looking for a clue. Something about my mother's mood made me sense there was a right and a wrong answer. Enchiladas, false? Tuna, true?

I walked back to the car. I said I guessed Captain Chowder's.

There was a ship's porthole in the door. The hostess led us to a driftwood table, then handed us parchment menus with purposefully charred corners.

"Don't look at the prices, Jill. Just order what you want."

In the dingy candlelight, I studied the menu, but before I

had a chance to savor my possibilities—the captain's tender young abalone, the mate's ocean-fresh golden-fried flounder—the waitress came over and my mother said, "We'll have two Australian lobster tail thermidors and a clam chowder for the baby."

She unfurled her rolled napkin as though cracking a whip, then smoothed it across her lap. "I don't care how much money we spend, kiddo. We're celebrating." She lifted her water glass. "To all the sales we're going to make."

We clinked rims. Our ice cubes rattled.

Then she jerked back her chair, excused herself, and went to the bathroom. I fed Pete a bread stick to keep him from fidgeting. When she came back, I could see she'd been crying.

The soup and lobsters arrived.

She started sawing into hers as if it was a grizzled chuck steak. "It's a little rubbery," she said, sighing.

I shrugged. Mine tasted good.

"And I should never have ordered the sauce. Why the fuck did I order a cream sauce? I mean, what's the point of eating lobster if you can't even taste it?"

I didn't say anything. I liked the sauce best. It tasted like Cheez Whiz.

"I'm really disappointed," she said, tapping her plate with her fork prongs. She chewed on a nail for a while rather than chew on her food, but in the end, with her nervous picking, she eventually cleaned her plate.

"You're not disappointed?" she asked incredulously, bunching up her napkin.

I said it wasn't that bad.

"Well, I don't know about you, but I'd like to try again."

She signaled the waitress for our check, then slapped down a twenty with disgust and herded us out into the noon glare. The food court looked drained of color. Heat bands made the painted stripes in the parking lot appear to levitate—a floating ideal of order above the gravel-strewn ground. For a moment, she pressed her palms against her temples and squeezed, then walked toward the Rusty Pelican.

"Table for three," she told the hostess. This restaurant was a lot smaller than Captain Chowder's, but it had the same basic motif—gauzy nets, lead anchors, and blanched driftwood. The hostess handed my mother a couple of red menus, but my mother brushed them aside.

"We want two lobster lunches," she said. "We want them broiled and we want them plain. No sauces, no cream, no buttery gunk you whip up in the kitchen. No nothing. Got it?"

The hostess suppressed a sigh, then shot a gaga glance over her shoulder. "I'll tell your waiter."

As soon as we were alone, I mentioned I wasn't all that hungry.

"Just eat what you want," she said. "We're supposed to be celebrating." She picked the sesame seeds off a cracker until the cracker's surface was as pocked as the moon's.

When the lobsters arrived, I made myself eat. I felt I had no choice. By the way my mother chewed, I could see she was forcing herself, too. She ate only half her tail, then poked around the shell, prying off the sticky pieces with the same vague annoyance she pried gum off the bottom of her shoe.

"Well, I'm finally satisfied," she said, nudging her plate aside, "aren't you?"

I said I felt a little ill.

"At least we got our money's worth, kiddo. At least we weren't taken this time."

But when our bill arrived and she paid for it with a credit card, her signature looked so listless, I doubt it made it through all the carbons.

That night, my mother's choice of motel was not celebratory—a dinky brown bungalow affair just east of San Diego. For no reason that I could fathom, the management had crammed the double bed halfway into the closet. When I looked up from my pillow, I saw a clothing bar and wire hangers.

"What do you think this is about?" I asked, staring up into the murky recesses. Pete was on my left, fast asleep. My mother was on my right, half-undressed, with a pillow over her eyes. She drew up her knees.

"Why was I such a fool?" she murmured. "Why was I such a gullible, stupid, idiotic fool to let myself get involved with him?"

I reeled around, desperate for company, but the pillow remained over her eyes; and that was all she said.

Sometime around midnight, I was jostled awake by the bounce of our mattress. Her lavender robe trailing, my mother disappeared into the bathroom. Assuming she went in there to cry again (my mother always cried in bathrooms), I waited a couple of minutes, then gingerly opened the door. She was standing naked under a hissing fluorescent (her robe a purple puddle around her feet), staring at the back of her calves. Red welts the size of saucers stippled her arms and legs.

"What do you think they are?" she asked.

I bent down, touching one of the lumps with my hand. An

83

uncanny mixture of heat and cold, like the slow burn of ice, radiated out of it. "Maybe it's some sort of reaction to the lobsters," I said.

"I don't think so. The rash started this morning." She covered her face with her hands. "I'm burning up, Jilly."

She said she was going to the emergency room and that I should stay there with Pete, try to get some sleep.

I didn't want to stay. I didn't want to put my head back in that closet without her. I said we were going, too.

Behind the wheel, she drove as if the freeway were banked weirdly or made up of sand and mirage. The hospital was only two off-ramps away, but she was drenched in sweat by the time we got there. An orderly led her into an examining room while Pete and I sat down on stiff plastic chairs. To keep him from crying, I let him crayon all over the hygiene brochures. When he got tired, I hauled him onto my lap and covered him with my mohair sweater.

Around 2:00 A.M., my mother was wheeled in by a nurse.

"We're not sticking around here," she whispered as soon as the nurse left. "They're giving me some cock-and-bull story about admitting me for tests." Her eyes looked glassy, bloodshot, feverish, crazed. "I told them I had you kids with me. Some busybody wanted Child Welfare to come fetch you. Just get us out of here, Jilly. Do you think you can drive home?"

I shrugged. I wasn't sure. I said I guessed I could.

"If you're not sure, you better say so now, kid."

My only real road time amounted to thirty hours in driver's ed—four kids crammed into a Valiant with a petrified gym teacher.

"I'm sure," I lied.

Without asking permission, I borrowed the wheelchair and trundled my mother to the car. I helped her into the front seat and laid Pete across the back. Without so much as glancing at a map, I slid in behind the wheel and started the engine. Black exhaust chugged out the tailpipe. I pumped the pedal a half dozen times to warm up the motor and my nerves. The car bucked along with my heart. I glanced at my mother.

She was slumped forward, snoring softly. In the pale glow of the dash, I couldn't see her rash, just a crescent of her face. A kiss curl lay plastered to her temple and her jaw was slung open. I smelled the sour, candied breath of fever.

I released the emergency brake and rolled over the exit bumps. The boulevard was empty. Under the yellow halos of streetlights, I practiced switching lanes, braking, the glide and pivot of steering. Only when I felt I had my car legs, did I head for the freeway.

It stood on stout concrete pillars. Even with my window shut, I could hear the rumble of traffic.

I started up the on-ramp, praying for a tiny opening amid the thundering semis. I gripped the wheel and floored the accelerator. Seconds later, when I found us unharmed, one car amid many, an indistinguishable animal in a big, moving herd, I felt heady exhilaration.

We were near the ocean and patches of fog, no denser than cigar smoke, drifted across the asphalt. Oncoming headlights flared, flashed, then crumpled into crystals as they passed. I grew hypnotized by their onrush, by the fog, by the rows of tiny reflectors, like glinting buttons, in the woolly moisture. From time to time, I had to shake my head and blink rapidly just to stay alert.

Near the 605 interchange, I must have momentarily dozed off because the steering wheel vanished and I was careening through a stockyard with semaphores flashing and big lobster red boxcars chugging in on me. I flew over some train tracks before I realized they were reflector bumps, snapped awake, and swerved back into my lane.

I missed a pickup by inches.

I couldn't stop trembling. I cranked open my window and turned on—no, blasted—the radio. I forced myself to sing along. I sang, "Somebody to Love," "Ain't No Mountain High Enough," "Baby You're a Rich Man." I belted out "Respect." Between songs, I read the billboards aloud: "Have a ball today in your Chevrolet."

My mother barely opened her eyes.

In the distance stood Torrance's factory stacks, sparking and smoking like so many chimney fires. I sped through their sulfuric air, the hissing power poles, the slumbering suburbs of Inglewood.

By the Santa Monica foothills, I had regained just enough confidence to steer with one hand and spin the green radio dial with the other. When the steep grade over the mountains began, I thwacked down the accelerator and barreled up in time to the music. When the road began twisting, I gracefully took the curves.

Somewhere between Los Angeles and the valley, between clear reception and unnerving static, the radio grew garbled, then died. A sudden golden silence reigned. We were coming over the crest of the mountains and the valley fanned out before us—a scintillation of lights so geometrically precise, they looked as if they'd been ruled into pink and violet dawn.

In all this tender light, my mother looked awful, but we were close enough to home for me not to panic. Besides, I was beginning to enjoy all this horsepower under my reign. It gave me a sense of total control I had never before experienced—and have rarely felt since.

That morning, Jack drove my mother to UCLA Medical Center where she spent the next ten days undergoing tests.

The doctors couldn't figure out what she had. But I knew. Once before, when a mustachioed Cadillac salesman she didn't even like dumped her, she'd broken out in hives. These were just bigger lumps for a bigger fall.

I missed her fiercely. The hospital was too far to walk to, so, mostly, we spoke on the phone. Her voice sounded hollow. Sometimes, after cradling the receiver, I was so overcome with anxiety it seemed to permeate my clothes and cling to my hair. I wasn't worried about my mother's health (by day two, the doctors said she'd be okay), I was worried about her vulnerability.

To keep us going, Jack worked after school for Mrs. Mc-Caffrey and Friday nights for an Italian baker. He learned to break eggs with one hand and whipped up cannoli so huge and ornate, they looked as if children had baked them in their dreams.

I wasn't quite so useful. Mrs. McCaffrey had fired me three weeks before. (During a furniture survey at Saks, she and the client had caught me napping on an antique display sofa, a velvet pillow over my eyes and my gladiator sandals up on the rosewood bolster.) I was now working at Whitefront, a discount department store.

Whitefront's slogan was: "The bigger the crowds, the bigger the discounts!" They'd recently added another full acre to their farm-size parking lot.

My job was to trek the hot asphalt every Saturday, stuffing "Discount of the day!" flyers under the windshield wipers of parked cars. I loathed the work and yearned almost wistfully for my soliciting days at the air-conditioned mall. The task of slapping flyers on cars seemed pointless. By dusk, all the leaflets had been thrown away anyhow. You could see them scuttling across the pavement in the ceaseless wind.

Mostly, I chucked the flyers in a Dumpster, then snuck to the far end of the parking lot and broke into cars. No one locked their doors in those days. I never stole anything more than bubble gum or Life Savers. Stealing wasn't the point. I wanted to see what other people had. I opened glove compartments, pumped accelerators, checked myself out in rearview mirrors. I sat in plush seats, lambskin seats, soft leather seats, hoping to catch a glimpse of myself against the luxurious fabric of a different destiny.

———†———

Then we met Lenny. My mother hadn't been out of the hospital two weeks when Mrs. McCaffrey introduced them. Lenny was a homely man with a salesman's hyperbolic patter and a cult leader's unyielding stare.

He owned a small, prosperous market-research company, Mrs. McCaffrey's main competition, but kindhearted Mrs. McCaffrey, worried about my mother's setback, knew Mom needed all the work she could get in the upcoming summer months. What Mrs. McCaffrey didn't know was how Lenny's firm kept mushrooming while her own business was flagging with the economy. Lenny was able to underbid his rivals because, when he couldn't finish a job on budget, he simply turned in fraudulent data.

He hired Mom, Jack, and me to make up the public's opinions. He didn't start us fudging polls right off, but eased us in slowly by lecturing us on what he called "Leonard's two market maxims"—number one, people have no opinions; number two, whoever controls the research comes out on top. He even prophesied a time when public-opinion polls would be the litmus test by which Americans judged reality.

Every weekend, working at his pink Formica kitchen table (Lenny had no office), we were to imagine ourselves as the Average American Family (a creative leap I could barely sustain) and fill out his questionnaires accordingly. Did we like Swanson TV dinners? If so, why? What color would we choose for our new Cadillac Coupe de Ville? Forest green? Autumn wheat? Midnight blue? On a scale of one to ten, how would we rate the new Talking Barbie? Arrow wax? Dr. Ross's dog food? What was our education? Our income? Our status?

Sometimes, I filled out the questionnaires as a senior citizen (my handwriting turned tremulous), a housewife (my print became prissy), a teenager (all smudges and pink erasures). We even forged signatures. I was a natural at it. The alphabet as abstract art. The greatest forgers are always illiterates and I was practically illiterate. Lenny encouraged me, and I, aching for any older man's praise, fell for his every compliment.

From the side, Lenny looked exactly like a short, red-headed Hitler—flat cranium, flat hair, a weak Roman nose, and a pint-size mustache. His dress style, however, nullified any reference to his look-alike. He wore flowered bell-bottoms and Nehru jackets, or cowboy boots and leather chaps, or Brooks Brothers suits, depending on his mood—and his mood was constantly changing.

Out in the field (Lenny made sure at least half of every poll was taken legitimately), his irreverence stunned and titillated me. He set up in shopping malls without permission, then dared managers to throw him out. He lied blatantly to clients, then rolled his eyes behind their backs.

Sometimes, when I showed up for work early, he called me his little protégé. Other times, he stood by the mall entry and screamed at me for wearing my hair ratted or my makeup smeared. He said I looked like a little slut and that he had an image to uphold and I was definitely, definitely dragging it down. Then, sighing deeply, he took out his silk handkerchief and, with bewildering tenderness, mopped up my runny mascara.

But mostly, it was his wantonness with money that captivated me. Lenny shopped in binges and bought on whim—every shiny gizmo that caught his eye: a battery-operated shoe polisher, night-vision binoculars, a musical doorbell, a toilet-seat warmer. If you were lucky enough to be around during one of his sprees, his boundless buying often spilled over onto you.

I didn't particularly like what he bought me. I didn't care for gizmos. Yet I was willing to abash myself and thank him profusely for the cheap gold lamé scarves and electric tooth-brushes. I needed to feel I was the kind of girl upon whom men lavished gifts.

One evening, he took Mom and me shopping for new uniforms. We didn't wear uniforms, but Lenny, on the spur of the moment, decided to revamp his image. He herded us into a Zody's and insisted we try on flowered schmatas and maxiskirts. The more outrageous the outfit, the more we sashayed and minced before him. But when he had us try on pink-aproned dresses that made us look like Swiss milkmaids, then jokingly suggested we yodel, my mother fell silent. I, however, yodeled.

Sometimes, for no reason whatsoever, he handed out fifty-dollar bills and called them bonuses. I quickly stuffed mine into my pocket with a sweaty palm.

Yet, when pay time came, more likely than not, his checks bounced. Before Lenny could go on another shopping spree, before the ink on his checks dried, my mother would lead Jack and me to the nearest bank to swap the paper for cash. Lenny usually pursued us as far as the bank door, berating us for our lack of trust, for ruining his good name. He said he thought we were like a family. I could see his hurt expression through the tinted window when the teller counted out our money—his eyes squinting, red brows knit, the bristles of his tiny Hitlerian mustache practically touching the glass.

———†———

One Saturday, Lenny, Jack, and I were forging questionnaires at our kitchen table when the doorbell rang. We were working at home because Lenny's kitchen was being painted.

I got up to answer the bell. From the stout shadow in the foyer glass, all bulk and blue suit, I thought it was Dad. I hadn't seen him in months. The two, three times he'd come over to pick up Tommy for an afternoon or to fight with my mother about money, I'd hidden in my room.

Steeling myself, I cracked open the door.

A fat man about my father's age stood sweating profusely on our shadeless stoop. He set down a scarred suitcase, then took out a wadded handkerchief and mopped up his brow. "Hey, princess, how ya doing today? Quite a hill you have here. A real schlepp. Folks around?"

"Sorry," I said. My mother had taken Tommy and Pete to the park so they wouldn't get on Lenny's nerves.

"I'm Mr. Ciment," Lenny said, coming up behind me.

"Well, Mr. Cement, can I borrow your ear for a couple of minutes?"

"Me ear *es su* ear," Lenny said. He winked at me.

"What I have in this suitcase could change your kid's life. Is she your only one?"

"I have nine children," Lenny said. "But Jilly Beans here is my favorite."

"Mind if I come in?" the man asked, a little stunned by his good fortune.

"Suit yourself," Lenny said.

The man hauled his suitcase into the living room, then knelt down beside it. He tried to open the latches, but his hands were too sweaty to get a solid grip. "I got the world in here, Mr. Cement. I got the whole world in here if I could just darn well get to it. Pardon my French, little lady." He took out a penknife and started jabbing the lock till it sprang.

A set of the *World Book Encyclopedia* bound in red imitation leather with gold embossed letters sat squeezed in his cheap suitcase. He pried one volume free with his thick fingers and handed it to me. *M*——*macaroni to myth.*

"You like?" he asked.

I nodded.

"Does it have pictures?" Lenny asked. "Because we're a picture-book family."

"Course it has pictures," the man said. "But it has much more than that, Mr. Cement. Much more. It has eighteen information-packed volumes *plus* a reading and study guide. Help those little ones get their homework done. Scholars write for us, Mr. Cement, real professors and scientists. Only the cream de la cream. We've been in business since 1917, and let me tell you—"

"I like pictures," Lenny said. "I like them big and I like them in color. I just asked if it had pictures."

The man sank back on his haunches, not sure if Lenny was kidding him.

"I'll tell you what, Mr. Cement, take a look for yourself. Princess, hand your dad that volume."

I gave Lenny volume *M.*

He sat down on the sofa and flipped through the pages. A hairy mammoth. A map of Manitoba. A malaria-carrying mosquito. Under "Mankind," he glanced for a moment at four illustrations captioned "How Mankind Differs from Animals." A sketchy outline of a big, wrinkled brain with $2+2 = 4$ inside: "Man has a greater brain capacity and can reason." A hammer, paintbrush, and awl: "Man has an opposable thumb and can use tools to create or change his surroundings." A badly drawn version of Rodin's *The Thinker:* "Man has a soul and can express noble ideas." A beautiful black-and-white rendering of van Gogh's *Starry Night:* "Man creates things of lasting hope and beauty."

Suddenly, I wanted these books with their paint-by-number truths, but I knew enough not to say it. If Lenny even sensed my yearning, he'd never buy them for me.

"I don't see anything in color," Lenny said, skimming through the rest of the pages.

"You want color pictures, we got color pictures," the man said. He stooped over his suitcase, pulled out another volume and began frenetically riffling through its pages.

Jack appeared in the doorway. "Jesus Christ, Lenny," he said, and left.

I wanted to leave, too. I felt awful for the man, but I didn't want to give up the encyclopedia. I honestly believed that if I owned it, kept those books lined up on my shelf in alphabetical order, all their knowledge would miraculously seep into me, like radiation, without my even reading them. Staring at their gold-leaf letters, I almost convinced myself that the only explanation for my getting *D*'s and *F*'s in school, the only reason I wasn't college-bound and would wind up working for Lenny for the rest of my life, or, worse, at a Woolworth lunch counter, was that I didn't own a full set of the *World Book Encyclopedia* with its red imitation leather bindings.

"Yep," Lenny said, "Daddy and his little girl go in for color pictures—the brighter the better. Right, Jilly?"

I didn't say anything.

"Right, Jilly Beans?"

"Right, Lenny," I mumbled.

"Honey, if I told you once, I told you a thousand times"—
he winked at me—"don't call me by my first name."

"Anything you say, Dad," I said.

———†———

That fall, when the glut of polls (both crooked and legit)
became too great for Mom, Jack, and me to handle alone,
Lenny hired three men to join us—John, Curly, and Louie. At
one time or another, each man had been Lenny's lover.

John was a lanky Englishman with an acrid feline wit; he
lashed out at everyone, mostly himself. Curly was slow-
witted to the point of exasperation. On stifling afternoons,
when he picked up Jack and me after school to drive us to the
mall in his clunker, he kept the windows rolled up so that
passersby would think he had air conditioning. Louie was a
sweet boy from Texas, a redheaded Gary Cooper, who con-
fided in me that he was into "golden showers." I thought that
meant he was into being rained on by money.

Each man was exempt from work as long as he was sleeping with Lenny. The instant the relationship soured, he was
back in the mall with the rest of us, clipboard in hand, taking
dictation from shoppers who pontificated about toilet paper or
Mr. Clean or chocolate-chip cookies.

Lenny never let his boys know about the shadier aspects of
his business. When a job fell behind schedule, he sent me to
the ladies' room to fudge surveys. Sitting in a locked stall, eyes
shut, I tried to envision the blank questionnaires until inspira-
tion struck—a medley of recollected radio jingles and cathode-
tube blue hallucinations. Then, pencil flying, I scribbled

responses as if they were being whispered to me by disembodied voices:

"My poodle is a picky eater, but Dr. Ross's dog food is dog-gone good."

"It's the tart, tangy homemade taste of Hunt's catsup that keeps me coming back."

"A wide-track Pontiac gives my large family living room comfort."

Some afternoons, having fabricated so many different opinions in so many various handwritings, I'd emerge from the dank bathroom into the bright mall lights not knowing who I was.

Just before Christmas, Lenny came up with the bright idea of buying a bus, equipping it with desks and electric pencil sharpeners, and renaming his business Voyager Research. This way, he could save on the cost of renting mall space. Besides, he'd pretty much alienated every mall manager in the valley and was running out of places. With a fully equipped bus, he could just pull up to the curb on, say, Hollywood Boulevard and rope in the tourists.

Since Lenny was incapable of saving, he needed a cheap deal. Once a year the California State Department of Correction auctioned off their old prison buses—big, lugubrious gray-and-white vehicles that looked, to me at least, like school buses. Lenny bought one sight unseen, then insisted we go with him to Chino State Penitentiary to pick it up. When John and my mother balked, he bribed them. He didn't have to bribe me, though. I wanted to see prison. I wanted to see anything outside the gaudy hues of a mall.

The penitentiary sat behind a thirty-foot-high cinder-block

fence. We never saw anything more than its parking lot. The lot didn't look any different from Whitefront's, save for the lack of scuttling flyers and shopping carts. Following Lenny across the asphalt, I suddenly experienced what the kids at school called "vu ja-de," the feeling that you'd never been anywhere.

Once in the bus, Lenny locked us in the prisoners' section. He brought along a padlock and while we were inspecting the seats, searching for sawed-off files, he slammed fast the barred door and clamped down the lock. John became furious. He stormed to the back of the bus and wouldn't speak to Lenny. Curly and Louie joined him. My mother sat down, inclined her head against a grungy barred window, and shut her eyes. But not Jack and me. We'd seen Paul Muni in *I Am a Fugitive from a Chain Gang*. We knew our parts. As Lenny piloted us down the freeway, we rattled the bars and stamped our feet. We made grotesque faces at passing motorists, then flailed with laughter. Whenever I spied a girl my own age looking bored in the rear seat of, say, a Lincoln Continental, I squashed my face against the iron bars and screeched, in a voice that even frightened me, "Let me out! Let me out!"

———†———

With his new mobility, Lenny polled the length and breadth of California. He was the first local company to offer a statewide service: "From Eureka to San Diego, state-of-the-art scientific data collected by our superior Voyager staff." The superior staff consisted of John, Curly, and Louie. At first, Lenny took only the men on trips. But they disappeared at night, got blotto, whisked hustlers in and out of their motel rooms. They were worthless by morning. My mother wasn't much more reliable. When her turn came, she snuck off during happy hour to check out the local singles bar scene or canceled at the last minute because Pete was running a fever. So by default, Jack and I became Lenny's traveling companions. After all, we had nowhere to go at night save for the dinky motel swimming pool with its icy water and floating dead wasps.

Jack was doing well in school and wouldn't travel during the week. But I saw no problem. Fridays (and sometimes Thursdays as well), I accompanied Lenny up and down Interstate 5. Though every destination looked alike—a shadeless mall parking lot with a lone photo kiosk, like a sundial, set in its center—I harbored the illusion that I was going places. When my mother objected to my missing class, I balked, cajoled, nagged, threw tantrums, said it was my only shot at earning *real* money. Said I was saving up for college.

It was a lie. But I liked the sound of it. I was failing nearly every subject in school and no one seemed to expect more, save for my mom and my old friend Rachel Zimmerman. One afternoon, my English teacher actually waved my scribbled, ill-conceived book report in front of the class and said, "Okay, Ciment, spell *cat. P, Q, R?*"

In a desperate attempt to jump-start me reading, my mother gave me soft-core pornography—*The Mouth Lover, Valley of the Dolls, Peyton Place*. She hoped it would catch my attention—it did. To keep me reading, Rachel gave me real novels—*Jane Eyre, The Magic Mountain,* and her favorite, *Siddhartha*. She even fed me children's classics so that I could catch up with my peers—*Charlotte's Web* and *White Fang*. I liked *White Fang* a lot more than *Siddhartha* but was too ashamed to tell her.

She and I were going to run away to Paris as soon as we turned eighteen. She was going to be a writer à la Simone de Beauvoir and I a painter à la Picasso. We spent hours envisioning our garret—slanted skylights, a view of the gray Seine, accordion music filtering in through the French windows. In the interim, her parents were taking her on a museum tour of Europe that summer, then enrolling her for one semester in a French exchange program. Rachel hinted that if she asked her parents nicely, they might invite me to tag along for the museum jaunt.

I knew they wouldn't. They hated me. I was the trash who got their daughter to smoke dope, ditch class, talk back. One day, Mrs. Zimmerman saw me polling with Louie and Curly at the Galleria, and when I waved, she looked through me, pretended I was part of the tacky decor.

I never mentioned the incident to Rachel. She believed her parents were glamorous, benevolent figures, Jewish versions of Scott and Zelda Fitzgerald with hearts as big as Albert Schweitzer's. When she took out the map of Europe and described all the art museums we were going to visit, I allowed myself to climb those imaginary marble steps, knowing full well I'd never see them.

My summer had already been spoken for. Lenny was going nationwide and wanted Jack and me to work a six-week stint in Chicago. (Obviously, Mom couldn't go because of the boys.) He promised to pay us top dollar and put us up in style—Ramada Inn with heated swimming pool, double beds, and color TV.

We talked things over with Mom. Jack had been accepted at UCLA and was desperate for money. I was just desperate. Having taken another scrape-by sales job for the summer, Mom thought this was our big opportunity to sock away a stash for our educations, not wind up selling schmatas like she did. She urged us to do it.

That evening, I called Rachel and told her not to bother talking to her parents, Europe had to wait, I had big plans of my own. I made the job sound as important as I could, all hush-hush research and a bottomless expense account. I prattled on about how much more of an education I'd get working in the real world rather than trudging through some old art museums. Rachel knew I was lying. After I hung up, I sat in my room with my knees drawn up. No one had done any gardening since Dad left and dead vines clotted the window. If I shut off my reading light, I could barely see my own feet. Through the open door, I could just make out a corner of my mural in Tommy and Pete's room. I must have used the wrong kind of paint because the animals were flaking off. Mom kept nagging me to repair them, but I didn't want to. In truth, I liked the mural better this way—the cracked paint made it look old and distinguished, as close as I was going to get to antiquity.

Rachel flew to Heathrow three weeks before I left for Chicago. At the last minute, she told me she was going to mail me a chocolate bar from every country in Europe she visited. She knew I loved chocolate and thought this was a heartfelt gesture.

I hated her for it.

Lenny was late picking us up for the airport. Jack and I had never flown before and we were anxious to get going. Lenny took surface streets, then dawdled in the airport's octagonal glass gift shop before sauntering up to the boarding gate two minutes before takeoff. The flustered blond airline rep had just given away our assigned seats to three hippie standbys and all that was left was a row of inflexible ones buttressed against the rear bathrooms.

Lenny became enraged. He called the rep a "cunt" and screamed for her supervisor. He brandished his One Hundred Thousand Mile Gold Card and threatened to have everyone fired. He said if his back went out because of the stiff seats, he'd sue the pants off the airline.

Before the supervisor arrived, the poor girl put us up in first class just to stop Lenny's ranting. By the way he grinned as we hurried through the gate, I could tell he'd pulled this one before.

Jack kindly let me have the window seat. I kept my cheek pressed against the pane, watching LA vanish under umber smog, then blue haze, then stringy gray clouds.

When my neck stiffened, I sat back and propped up my thonged feet on the leather footrest. A ponytailed stewardess handed out cream-colored menus that looked like wedding invitations. After much pondering, I opted for the bacon-wrapped filet mignon, potatoes au gratin, and marble cake. When the stewardess said I could have two desserts, I was flabbergasted. I took gulps of Lenny's free champagne and arrived at O'Hare tipsy and nauseous.

I rode in my first taxicab, streaking past the manicured lawns of suburban Chicago to a red-roofed Ramada Inn. I tipped a pimply bellhop to lug my cardboard suitcase to the room. I stretched out on the pilled bedspread and, despite my not being hungry, ordered french fries from room service (after all, Lenny had promised us room service). I ate a couple of crisp ones, then chucked the rest into the wastebasket. I snapped on the color TV, dug into my purse and fished out a candy bar Rachel had sent me. It was called Côte-d'Or and she'd labeled it "France." I jammed the whole thing into my mouth and chomped on it until nothing remained but a saccharine aftertaste.

Eden Plaza was suburban Chicago's pride, a mall as big as a small town. It even had its own police force.

Every morning save Sunday, Lenny dropped Jack and me off by the main entrance, a bank of tinted glass doors under a wing-shaped red canopy. Jack opened the polling center while I ate breakfast at White Castle or Ice Cream World or Jolly Rogers. I was crazy about spending my per diem.

Our job was to interview pregnant women. After the shoppers started arriving, I scoured the mall for expectant mothers, from ponytailed teenagers to muumuued housewives. When I gathered up two or three, Jack led them to a windowless room and showed them slides of package prototypes, featuring black infants on pink and blue labels.

The respondents were all white. The survey was being sponsored by a diaper company to test its new packaging. The poll asked about the design's impact, mass appeal, and style, but purposely made no mention of the baby's race. It didn't need to; the unspoken question was clear. Would a white woman buy a bag of diapers with a black baby on it? Or, for that matter, would a black woman, tired of never seeing a black infant on any package, be grateful for the company's token effort and buy its product in droves? The survey's race quotas were split down the middle—half the respondents were supposed to be white, the other half black.

In the two weeks I'd been combing Eden Plaza for expectant mothers, I'd never even seen a black person, let alone a pregnant one. Lenny said not to worry, that we'd fill in the "black" questionnaires ourselves.

Every evening, after the last batch of respondents left, Jack locked the door and we plopped down on their still-warm chairs to fill in a couple of "black" responses. Lenny figured we needed a mixed sampling on hand in case the client ever dropped by.

One Friday afternoon, the client did drop by, a stocky, bulldog-jowled man and his buzz-cut assistant. Jack stalled them outside while I, in a frenzied panic, hid any phony-looking forged surveys. Then I snuck out the rear door and tried to call Lenny. I dialed the Ramada Inn and had the operator page his room, the pool, the lobby, the Tiki Bar, but, as usual, Lenny was nowhere to be found.

When I got back, Jack was giving the clients a tour. The older man had his hand on Jack's shoulder and was nodding in gung ho approval, while his assistant, shifting from Oxford to brown Oxford, tried to stifle an enormous yawn. Even from where I stood, on the far side of the silver escalator, I could hear Jack lying to them with a brazen mendacity that would have made Lenny proud.

After that, as an added precaution, Lenny put aside Tuesday and Wednesday mornings to forge the "black" question-naires at the motel.

With the sun striking the olive green drapes of our ad-joining rooms, Jack and I filled in responses as Delilah, Lu-cille, or Jane, black women on their first, second, or seventh pregnancy.

For some inexplicable reason, I never felt closer to my brother than when we took on the personae of these pregnant women. Our sibling bickering ceased, and I helped him juice up his pedestrian forging, while he, without a hint of disdain, corrected my impossible spelling.

Then, in dorky trunks and a firecracker red bikini, we snuck out to the pool to take a dip before Lenny whisked us off to the mall. The pool plashed beside a thruway, its turquoise surface wrinkled by constant wind. Jack shivered on the tiled edge, dipping a white toe into the tepid water before easing himself in—foot to ankle to knee to thigh, until his face, two blown-up cheeks of locked breath, glided beneath the surface. He wasn't nearly as strong a swimmer as I, but on those mornings, I gladly demurred to my big brother and swam in his wake.

Then Jack went back to LA. He'd preenrolled for a sum-mer school chemistry course and had to leave after the fourth week. I waved good-bye to him at Eden Plaza. For the next couple of hours, I played at being a mysterious lone traveler and thought about myself in the third person: "Dauntlessly, she walks the mezzanine of this futuristic Plexiglas and steel city. . . ." Then I sank into a well of loneliness without him.

Lenny hired a couple of local girls to work the legitimate end of the survey, but these girls and I had nothing in common.

Linda Sosinski wanted to be a Carmelite nun and Toni McGinnis dreamed of having "loads and loads" of kids. Mostly, I ate alone, took breaks alone, polled alone, then returned to the Ramada Inn and swam alone, scouring the bottom of the pool for earrings and coins. "Selflessly, she combs the ocean depths for the lost Atlantis treasure that will save mankind. . . ." Afterward, I lay on the cold concrete, shivering in puddled effigy, watching the sky darken from sepia to lead to depthless violet.

When my mother called, I never told her how lonely I was. Instead, I prattled on about the thrill of room service or told her funny anecdotes about the girls Lenny hired (Linda Sosinski, despite her pious plans, wore leopard panties). And while I was speaking to my mother, I believed I was having a good time. Then I hung up and stared at the wallpaper, or the olive green drapes, or the stucco swirls, like tiny tornadoes, in the low ceiling.

Sometimes, when I couldn't sleep, I wandered the motel corridors, stepping over room-service trays to listen at closed doors. Since what I craved was human contact, I invariably wound up at the Tiki Bar. Or outside it. I was too young to go in.

The Tiki Bar was the motel's hot spot, a bamboo-paneled room with rattan tables, plastic palms, and a lounge act. The act was billed on a cardboard poster in the lobby—Lori Vega, "fresh from a six-month smash run in La Grange," and Bill Boxer, "her piano man extraordinaire." Lori was photographed in a low-cut sequined gown, holding a microphone to her breast like a corsage. Bill was snapped winking at the camera.

I sat in a big overstuffed chair behind a fern in the lobby and listened.

"Is anyone here tonight from the Big Apple?" Silence. "Cincinnati?" Zilch. "Peoria?" A couple of hoots and whistles. "Well," Bill said, "this is one for you farm boys."

The chugga-chugga, hiss, boom, bang of the electric congas began and Lori, her silver sequins flashing past the door, stepped onto the stage and crooned in a pitch-perfect, awful voice: " 'Che*rish* . . . is . . . the . . . word . . . I . . . use . . . to . . . describe allthefeelingsthatIhavehidingherefor you—*who—ooo—ooo—oOO—OOO—ooo* inside . . .' "

Sadness came over me—a sadness so huge, I knew it didn't come from the congas, or the singer, or my loneliness, but from something beyond the Ramada Inn—the air, or the night, or the spin of the earth and my own weak hold on it.

I returned to my room and snapped the color TV on and off, on and off, on and off, until I felt as if I was vanishing into an ever-shrinking cathode-tube blue dot.

———†———

Lenny and I lay sprawled on chaise longues by the pool. It was the first Sunday after Jack had left. The sun was at its zenith. Lenny was humming to himself, slathering coconut butter on his bright pink shins. I lay facedown, sullen and testy. For the past couple of days, all I had been able to think about was how to tell him I was quitting, but my only reason—dire loneliness—sounded so maudlin, I knew Lenny would use it to belittle me.

He shifted his leg, adjusted the tight elastic of his red bathing briefs, and in the bright, unflinching sunlight, I saw a sliver of his scrotum pop out. The skin was pulled taut, pocked with black hairs, pinched by his briefs. The testicle looked shiny, a ripe water blister on his inner thigh.

I couldn't take my eyes off it.

That night, Lenny seemed less formidable. Over dinner, I told him I didn't think I could finish out my stint in Chicago.

"Really, Jill?" he said, cutting into his T-bone. "Why is that?"

"No reason," I mumbled, "I just want to go home."

He rolled his eyes heavenward. "Well, I won't hear of it."

I said I didn't care what he would hear of. I was quitting.

He bunched up his napkin. "You ungrateful little cunt," he said.

I jerked back my chair, rattling his scotch on the rocks. I said I'd do what I wanted, that I wasn't his slave. Said if he hadn't heard already, it was a free country.

"Jilly Beans, sit," he said.

"I'm leaving, Lenny, and you can't stop me."

"You ungrateful little bitch," he said.

I ate alone in my room, a half a dozen salty snacks from the motel's vending machine. Sometime around ten, he knocked on my door. I pretended I wasn't in. I sat in the murky darkness, plucking teeny fluff balls off my pilled bedspread.

"I'm sorry, Jill. Open up. Please."

"Why should I?"

"Just do it," he said.

I cracked open the door.

"I thought you were having a good time in Chicago," he lied, bulling his way past me. He snapped on the lights and filched a couple of pretzels from a bag on the bureau. Then he skimmed his finger over the bureau top, dusting the tip with spilled salt, and licked that off, too. "I thought you liked traveling."

"I'd hardly call this traveling."

"What can we do to make this fun for you, Jilly? You know I can't work this job without you."

"I want to go home," I said. "I miss my mom and brothers."

"Why don't you buy them gifts?" He took out his wallet, thick with twenties, and plucked out five. He made a little fan of them on the bedspread.

"I can't believe you think I can be bought, Lenny."

Sighing loudly, he took out five more, making a second fan on the bed. "The job's been extended. I need you for three more weeks," he said flatly.

"No way."

He laid out a third fan, then threw an extra twenty on top.

The choice between money and its consequence, abject loneliness, was too great; I began to cry.

"Jesus fuck, Jill," he said, chucking down another hundred.

I was sobbing uncontrollably now, hiccuping into the bunched hem of my T-shirt.

He upped the ante, doubling the next fan.

Suddenly my tears, as real and stinging as they had been, transmuted into the saline solution that actresses use to do their big scene. I let them roll down my cheeks. For a moment, I felt the thrilling fusion of mastered performance and mad melodrama. I wasn't entirely in control, but I knew enough not to stop.

"I really, *really* miss my mom—I don't think I can handle this," I sobbed. I squeezed out more tears with the heels of my hands, all the while keeping a close eye on his wallet. I hiccuped and sniffled on cue. Finally, I was so moved and confused by my own performance, I no longer needed to act.

"What if we make it an even thousand?" Lenny sighed.

"This isn't about money," I muttered.

"Of course not," he said, dealing out a last stack of bills.

As tempted as I was, I didn't count the cash. I didn't even look at it. I let it sit there, rustling in the air conditioner's breeze.

"I'll see you tomorrow, then?" Lenny asked, scrutinizing my wet, blotchy face. "Nine sharp?"

I shrugged.

"Bright and bushy-tailed?"

"I guess so."

"That's my little protégé," he said.

As soon as Lenny left, I scooped up the twenties. I couldn't believe what had happened. I was tempted to toss them into the air, but I didn't dare—one might accidentally sail under the bureau where I couldn't reach it. Instead, I laid them out on the mattress in ten meticulous piles. I licked the tip of my thumb and counted them, savoring the sound—the pop of crisp paper. I grabbed the tenth stack, then drew it to my lips like a lover and kissed it. I flopped down amid the rest but, in no time, was too antsy to lie still.

I got up and paced the carpet. Anxious to celebrate, I dialed room service but hung up. I wasn't hungry. Next I tried my mom but she wasn't home. I peeked out the door to see if anyone was around to talk to, but all that lined the hall were the usual piled-up plates with a Camel butt floating in some un-touched consommé.

111

I shut the door and turned on the TV. I needed to hear human voices. I sat in its jittery blue light, staring at the screen, then the wallpaper and ceiling.

After awhile, I pushed aside the olive green drapes and peered out. The sky was ink black. I had to cup my eye to the glass to blot out my reflection. A parking lot receded as far as I could see. Moths, like ghostly soap flakes, wheeled around the arc lamps. There wasn't a soul in sight.

Feeling a surge of incontestable desolation, I closed my eyes and mashed my brow against the cold window. Then I decided to go down to the Tiki Bar. Or outside it. I rubbed off my runny mascara and turned away, heading out the door, while the other Jill, my mirrored image, also rubbed off her runny mascara and turned away, heading into the depths of a Ramada Inn parking lot.

When I got home, I was determined to squirrel away my earnings. Our neighborhood bank displayed a full-color poster in its squeegee-clean window—a generic dad snoozing on a burgundy red La-Z-Boy with grass green dollar signs sprouting around him. "Let your money grow for you!" the caption read. I opened a savings account so that my money could grow, too. But in no time, I was dipping into it—a ten spot here, a twenty there—until I filled up an entire bankbook with daily withdrawals. The tellers soon knew me by my first name.

I didn't mean to squander my savings. I had intended it to buy me a future devoid of Lenny and malls. I listened to my classmates prattle on about *their* prospects. Senior year had barely begun, and they were already discussing their futures with a pinpoint assuredness that left me dumbfounded. They knew which college they wanted to attend, which sorority they were going to pledge, the kind of guy they aimed to marry, the type of tract house they expected to buy, right down to the pattern of wallpaper they'd slap up in the guest's bathroom.

When I envisioned my future, I saw a fuzzy artist's palette enveloped in a thick, soupy fog. Or Lenny.

That fall, I worked for him every day after school and on the weekends. Jack occasionally joined me, but now that he was in college, he worked as little as possible and mostly for Mrs. McCaffrey. He said even if she didn't pay as much, she made him less nuts than Lenny. Mom agreed. She'd also quit Voyager Polls for good, taken a pay cut to keep regular hours and be home more with the boys. I stuck it out with Lenny. I'd tasted the good life in the guise of a per diem and I wanted "things." Lenny only encouraged me.

One day after work, I saw a lipstick red MG midget for sale. It was parked outside the mall and had chrome hubcaps as bright as suns. Lenny insisted on going with me to buy it. We pretended he was my father so that he could dicker the seller down. He told the astonished couple, a florid-faced ex-marine and his skeletal-thin wife, that I'd spent the summer picking strawberries in Calexico to save up for it. We got the car for a hundred and fifty dollars. It came without a roof and had a rusted dent the size of a man's fist in the passenger door. It didn't matter. I loved the car. I loved it as another kid might love a mangy dog.

Once a week, with a fastidiousness I never applied to my own person, I scrubbed and polished it, using saddle soap for its cracked seats, Windex for its chrome.

The Avengers, a British television show, was extremely popular in those days. The heroine was a stunning spy. She dressed in slinky outfits, karate-chopped Communists as humongous as bears, never perspired, and owned an MG midget like mine. Sometimes, when I was far from home and sure that no one knew me, I'd pull into a gas station and say, "Filler ep" in a British accent.

I drove my car to school, but, of course, I couldn't bear to stay. After one class—algebra, say—whatever pact I'd made with myself to try harder dissolved and I stared at the foot-long formulas being scribbled across the blackboard as one might stare at a spreading rash. I wanted to understand. I wanted to flop down on the quad with the other girls and sigh, "Wasn't yesterday's homework a bummer!" But after spending so much time with Lenny, the fragile hold I had on school gave way. The nanosecond the bell rang for class, I snuck off through a hole in the cyclone fence to my dented, roofless sports car and screeched off. Sometimes, I drove the exact routes my mom and I had taken to escape my father. Other times, I'd venture as far as Zuma Beach, light up a joint, and watch the tar green waves, all marbled with phosphorescence, somersault toward me.

To justify my ignorance, I scoffed at the idea that an artist needed to know anything as pedestrian as high school algebra. With my meager math, I tallied up the fact that I probably earned more at my summer job than my teachers did at theirs.

But I couldn't fool myself entirely. To give myself a semblance of a future, I began taking private art lessons. I found the names of my potential "masters" in the telephone book— the Studio School of French Impressionist Art, San Fernando Valley League of Flower Painters, Reseda Academy of Art. Sometimes my mother saw an art class advertised on the supermarket bulletin board and brought the flyer home for me— Beginning Still Life, Intermediate Still Life, Advanced Still Life, Portraits for Fun!

In dinky storefronts and rebuilt garages, dizzy from the acrid smell of turpentine, I listened with unwavering attention to these goateed men and smocked women, even when I sensed their aim at art was feeble.

I was instructed to "Paint in one breath!" "Pick colors that express your feelings about fruit." "Treat the canvas like a mirror." "A window." "A battlefield." "A dream." "A blank mind."

Saturday mornings, brush in hand, I stood before blue vases filled with yellow sunflowers, or pink bowls piled with red apples and purple grapes. (Sometimes the fruit was so old that mold grew out from under the pieces.) Behind each still life set up hung the obligatory velveteen sheet bunched in such a way that it had more folds than a pleated skirt.

I didn't care what was put in front of me—I painted to escape my fate with Lenny. I drew with a forger's ardent attention to detail. Degas said, "One has to commit a painting the way one commits a crime."

———†———

I was speeding home from school one day when I spotted a large black-and-red painting in a gallery window. It was hanging amid chintzy antiques and silk-screened seascapes. I stopped the car to study it. Under a sheen of varnish, a pile of toys— rag dolls, fire trucks, tin soldiers—appeared to be made out of motion and light. When I cupped my eye to the window glass to find the source of the painting's intensity, the toys imploded into sheer pigment.

It wasn't the first time I'd seen first-rate painting. Before Rachel went abroad, she and I had haunted the LA County Museum of Art whenever I could lure her into ditching class. I'd practically memorized the glimmering Manets and Monets from which the ladies at the Studio School of French Impressionist Art made their sallow copies. But I always assumed that art, real art, was the exclusive work of the museumed dead.

That afternoon, I made my mother call the gallery to see if the artist gave lessons. The woman who answered the phone was the artist's wife. She said he taught private drawing classes, but when my mother mentioned my age, the woman voiced trepidations about my working with nude models. I begged my mother to phone the artist himself, then slunk into my room— I was too shy to call on my own. A couple of minutes later, she appeared in the doorway.

"He sounds sweet, even charming," she said, brushing back my frizzy bangs with her stubby nails. "Your seeing naked models didn't seem to faze him at all, if it was okay with me. I said frankly I thought it was healthier than painting moldy fruit."

That Monday evening, I filled a tackle box with kneaded erasers, india ink, Speedball pens, and Conté crayons. I sharpened all my HB pencils until their points were as long as stalactites. I didn't want to seem amateurish or unprepared.

The class was held on the top floor of a run-down office building in Beverly Hills. A brass placard on the building's facade read, THE ARTIST AND WRITER'S HOUSE. I started up the dank stairs, envisioning budding Jack Londons scribbling away behind closed doors, where, in reality, middle-aged TV writers sat typing *I Dream of Jeannie* and *Mod Squad* scripts.

The class was in session when I got there. Two men and ten ladies sat bent over charcoal drawings. Even besmudged and ink-stained, the ladies had the same moneyed veneer as Rachel's mother. The two men wore white Top-Sider deck shoes. The artist stood gazing over their shoulders with a look of abject boredom. When he realized I was standing there, he turned around and smiled, but I was too shy to smile back.

I stared down at my thonged feet (his feet were sandaled, too!) and thanked him—a little too profusely—for letting me attend.

"You're very welcome," he said.

I kept my eyes riveted to the floor.

"Jill, isn't it? With an odd last name?"

"Ciment," I mumbled. "Pronounced like *concrete.*"

"Well, Miss Ciment pronounced like *concrete,* why don't you take a seat and we'll see what you can do."

I went straight to a drawing bench and straddled it, unfurling my rolled paper. The model lay posed on a wooden platform, hand on thigh, neck swiveled, torso as twisted as a rag being wrung out. His penis was uncircumcised. I could stare at it to my heart's content under the guise of being an art student. But, in truth, I didn't feel a hint of eroticism for my first naked man. Under the glaring spotlight, contorted in his impossible pose, the model looked, to me at least, as lifeless as a pink bowl of withered fruit.

What did arouse me, however, was the artist. He was in his mid-forties, gray-templed, with a scruffy black beard and heavy square glasses like the kind Clark Kent wore to hide his otherworldly good looks.

Now and again, he scuffed over to my bench and squinted at my effort. I had sketched everything—feet, calves, thighs, stomach, chest, neck, elbows, hands, except genitalia. It's not that I hadn't looked: I'd scrutinized its every fold, pucker, and hair. It was just that if I stumbled over my drawing, I didn't want to fall there.

"Not bad," he said.

Then he demonstrated, by lightly touching my arm, the way art worked. He traced with a paint-stained fingernail all the muscles leading in and out of my elbow. (It felt as if he were caressing me under my skin.) He told me that art was made up of tensions, overlappings, juxtapositions, not accuracy. He said truth and accuracy were not necessarily the same thing. He opened a huge ink-splattered book—*Italian Renaissance Drawings*—and broke down the fleeting geometry holding together Michelangelo's enormous athletes. Then he showed me what worked and didn't work in my sketch, kindly never mentioning the blank spot in the center.

When he finally scuffed off to help another student, a pear-shaped lady whose cheek was a hodgepodge of charcoal and rouge, I willed him to come back.

Next Monday, I showed up for class ridiculously early. The room was empty except for the model, a bleach-blond woman this time, who lounged in a pink bathrobe on the model stand, unshaven legs astride, furiously smoking a Pall Mall. The drawing benches were circled around her like Conestoga wagons around a campfire. When the artist finally walked in, he looked distracted. He nodded at the model, then at me, as if he barely recalled who I was, whereas I, during the course of the week, had committed to memory our every fleeting exchange. I took a seat on a far bench, sharpening my pencils until their points glistened. I thought I could lure him back to me with my raw drawing ability.

In those years, my love of art was confused with my wanting, at any price, recognition and praise. I brandished my talent with the same unabashed pride young girls flaunt their bodies. That evening, whenever he came near me, I drew wildly, fervently, sensually, not just to make an object of ardor but to become an object of ardor.

And because I didn't understand what I was doing, I felt awful about my tawdry sketches, my clumsy attempts at flirtation. But I didn't stop. Couldn't stop. In indelible ink, each drawing rendered the undeniable evidence of my longing.

After class, I berated myself for my poor work, for my all-too-obvious mooning glances. I wasn't a flirtatious girl, but I was coy in the way the shy are coy, in halting stares and scalding blushes.

One night, I arrived for class just as the artist was unlocking the door. He invited me to join him on the model stand and share his flat Coke until the other students showed up. I sat down inappropriately close to him. The Santa Ana was gusting. The air was hot, ion-charged. Whenever he took a gulp from the can, he leaned back and his forearm graced my bare shoulder. The blond down on my arms stood up. He wasn't wearing his usual undershirt and I could see a faint dusting of gray hair around the base of his throat. He looked "lived," and I wanted him all the more because of it.

From that night on, whenever I was supposed to be paying attention in school or roving the mall for Lenny, I'd fall spellbound by the escalator, say, and fantasize *our* affair: During class, he steals up to me and presses his bristly beard against my burning ear, asking me—no, *imploring* me—to stay after the others leave. When the last matron waddles out, he takes me in his arms and runs his hands over my throat, arms, face, breasts. We never speak. (I borrowed the scene from soft-core pornography where dialogue was scarce.) He slowly, deftly unbuttons my peasant blouse, peels down my hip-hugger bell-bottoms. He strokes me gently, almost teacherly, because I'm a virgin. We topple naked onto the pillowy model stand, kissing wildly. The actual sex act is vague, all fog and fade-out. But afterward, things are crystal clear. He loves me, and not just for my youthful body. I'm special and he knows it. He promises to leave his wife and—

A change in the Muzak jars me back to the mall and I stand blinking and confused beside the humming, ceaseless escalator.

———†———

A popular fad in those days was to write your boyfriend's name in masking tape on your midriff, then bask in the sun. It was the schoolgirl's equivalent of the sailor's tattoo. (Over the course of a semester, some fickle midriffs held the ghosts of so many boys' names, they read like faded pages from a telephone book.)

Obviously, since Arnold was thirty years older than I, married with two teenage children, emblazoning his name on my stomach wasn't exactly the thing to do. Besides, the girls who practiced this craze were pompom girls and twirlers, kids so far removed from my taste and temperament, we barely acknowledged one another's presence, let alone spoke.

Yet, I understood their madness. Had I been able to do it in secret, I would have stenciled his name on my body in a handwriting that was unquestionably my own.

One afternoon, Lenny phoned with what he said was good news. He'd just landed the P&G account and that meant a big bonus for me. The rub was it also meant traveling. I'd have to miss school.

"It's never bothered me before," I said, feeling sick at the thought of another motel room, a new mall.

"It's a ten-weekend job. You'd leave every Friday morning and not get back till late Monday night."

"Sorry," I said. "I can't miss Mondays."

"Why? You've got a big home economics exam?"

"I'm taking art lessons," I said.

"Really, Jill, let's put things in perspective. You're sixteen years old. You have your whole life to take art lessons."

"Lenny, find someone else. I can't go on Mondays."

"But I need you, Jilly Beans. No one's got your magic touch. Besides, you'll see the whole country. Did I mention it was a different city every week?"

"Lenny—"

"Guess which cities. I've got the list in front of me."

"Lenny—"

"Okay, I'll give you a clue. Jazz, bayous, scrumptious Cajun food."

"Find someone else."

"We both know I can't 'find someone else.' We both know *exactly* how these jobs get done. Don't let me down, Jill, when I'm about to land the biggest client of my life."

"It's not my problem," I said.

"Oh, yes it is. You quit now, honey, you quit forever. Don't think you're coming back. And, frankly, I can't see my little Jilly Beans flipping hamburgers for two bits an hour now that she's gone first class."

"I'm not going."

"Then we have nothing else to say."

"I guess not."

He slammed down the phone.

Over the next couple of days, I expected Lenny to call again, dangle some shiny promise before me to mesmerize me into going. Whenever our phone trilled, I hung back, steeling myself against his beguiling fast talk.

But he never called.

In no time, I was out of money. My mother could hardly pay for art lessons. Every morning, I scanned the want ads, but Lenny had my number—I wouldn't, couldn't, get myself to flip hamburgers. I called Mrs. McCaffrey, but she didn't have any work for me. Concerned as always, though, she gave me the number of a new polling firm. She said she'd never met the two gals who ran it but the word was that they were young and aggressive, real upstarts. She said this with a tinge of pained wistfulness. I brought the two ladies my resumé, upping my age to nineteen. They were ex-Chicagoans and impressed by the fact that I'd worked Eden Plaza. Both women had shed their midwestern accents and acquired tans that looked as if they'd been lacquered on.

To start me off, they gave me a simple, no-nonsense job. I was to work the North Valley Mall, interviewing girls, ages sixteen to twenty-one, about their preferences in perfume. Flowery or musk? Bottle or atomizer? What sample fragrance evoked which name? Tropical Nights. Allure. White Rose. Storm. It was the kind of job I could have done in my sleep, but between my heady infatuation and the sultry scents, whole hours passed with me slipping from one daydream into another.

To make up for lost time, I employed Lenny's technique, a legitimate questionnaire followed by a forged one. But after a Saturday or two, even that seemed like too much effort. I drove to the beach and filled in the rest of the questionnaires myself.

I thought I did a terrific job, far better than the inarticulate teenagers I was interviewing at the mall.

To protect myself, I had my fictitious girls refuse to give their names or phones numbers, claiming they didn't want their parents to know they squandered their allowances on perfume or hung out at the mall. But I had to come up with a few legitimate names. I used Rachel's, knowing she was safely out of the country. I threw in a dozen of my classmates', then phoned them later to ask them to cover for me.

I let another Saturday slip by before turning in the job; I didn't want it to look too easy. My new bosses were pleased; I was the first pollster to finish. Marcy, the scrawnier of the two, quickly skimmed through my questionnaires. "At least you know how to probe," she said, sighing. "The other girls don't even try to get detailed answers." I sighed along with her at the sad fact that their other employees did such slipshod work. She asked me if I would be free the following weekend and offered me a new assignment, a survey about imported cars.

"I own an MG midget," I said.

"Well, it should be right up your alley."

I took the surveys home, intending to employ the same

methods: Two days later, Marcy called. She sounded irate. She had done a spot check, discovered that one of the girls I had supposedly surveyed was living in France, and that according to her parents the girl had been living in France for the past two goddamn months!

I knew she was talking about Rachel.

"I don't know what you're up to, cookie, but you've got some big-time explaining to do. I'm going over the rest of your surveys with a fine-tooth comb and I better not find any other discrepancies. You be in my office tomorrow morning at nine sharp. Got it. Nine sharp."

Mom was out for the evening, so I banged on Jack's door and told him everything. "I feel ill, really ill," I said. "Oh, God, Jack, if she's angry about Rachel being in France, just wait till she goes through the other questionnaires. Half the girls don't exist. Except for that, though, I really did a good job."

"Did you put down any fake phone numbers?" he asked.

"I'm not stupid."

"Then they can't prove anything. All they have is one falsified survey. They can't throw you in jail for that."

"What if they find out about the others?"

"They won't."

"They might."

"Call Lenny. He'll know what to do."

"I don't want to call Lenny, Jack. I want him out of my life."

"Okay, tomorrow morning just prostrate yourself before the two ladies and beg for forgiveness."

I started to cry.

"I'll call Lenny," he said.

A couple of minutes later, he came back into the room. I

was curled up on his bed, eyes shut, clutching a pillow. "What did Lenny say?" I asked.

"Well, after he finished laughing, he said he knew the two ladies from his old Chicago days. They were bitches on wheels, but he thought he could smooth things out. He'll meet you there tomorrow morning."

Next day, I waited in the reception area while Lenny talked to the women. I tried to eavesdrop, but all I could hear was the blood banging in my ears.

Lenny finally sauntered out of their office. "Let's go," he said. "It's taken care of."

"What did you say to them?"

He nudged me toward the door, rolling his eyes in exasperation. "Not here, Jill," he muttered.

In the parking lot, I insisted he tell me.

"What do you think I said?"

"I don't have a clue, Lenny."

"Guess."

"I'm young and they should forgive and forget."

He laughed. "Hardly, Jill."

"Then what?" I said.

"I told them Rosie's—"

"Rachel's."

"*Excusez-moi.* I told them Rachel's parents were liars."

"You didn't."

"I most certainly did. I said their daughter was a runaway and they didn't have a clue where she was. I said you interviewed her at the mall with all the other bedraggled runaways."

"The ladies believed you? Rachel's parents are big-shot psychiatrists."

"That's exactly why they believed me." He opened his car door, then squinted over the vinyl roof. "An ice cream to celebrate your pardon?"

I didn't want to be in his debt any more than I was.

"I'm not hungry," I said.

"My treat."

I shook my head no.

"*Pul*-e-e-ease."

"Lenny, I'm not hungry."

"I insist," he said.

Over an opulent sundae I couldn't even swallow, he started right in on me like I knew he would. "Now will you return to work? Don't worry, it's a local job. I won't ask you to give up your precious Monday nights."

I poked at my ice cream, pretending to mull it over, but, in truth, I didn't think I had a choice.

Rachel came home from France aping Leslie Caron's coltish gait, Simone Signoret's husky, savvy, lived-too-long sighs. She'd been attending Lycee Le Grand and living with a Parisian family. Every sentence she uttered was peppered with French. It was *moi* this, *merci* that. All our old haunts—Du Par's, Café Figaro—now struck her as plastic and provincial. Even smoking marijuana wasn't as profound a high as smoking hashish, evidently the drug of choice for l'étudiante française.

When I told her about my fiasco with her parents and the perfume survey, she dismissed it as all part of American capitalism. She quoted Godard and Mao. She said with all I had going for me, she couldn't understand why I'd choose to work in anything as corrupt as market research.

After school, when I wasn't knee-deep in corruption, I practiced sketching Rachel. She was a zaftig girl more reminiscent of Renoir's apple-cheeked debutantes than the Parisian waif she aspired to be. Posed on her mother's chaise longue, naked save for a Gauloise dangling from her lips, she studied for her SATs while I made gesture drawings of her restless legs. She planned on attending Berkeley before soaring off to the Sorbonne and she wanted me to go with her. She said she'd share her monthly allowance with me. Said her parents had more money than was good for them; what they didn't know wouldn't hurt them. Said when she thought about all the poverty in the world, she hated her parents' money.

While I listened and drew, the afternoon rays bounced off her turquoise pool and lulled me. The tall glasses of lemonade, iced and sweetened by a silent maid, then spiked with Tanqueray gin stolen from Mr. Zimmerman's cabana bar, obliterated all fears of my uncertain future. I never told Rachel how I envied her this perfect calm. Sometimes I even let myself believe her. Then the gin wore off and I was back in inflexible reality.

I knew Paris was out of the question for a girl like me. I made up my own dream. As soon as I saved up enough money, I was moving to Greenwich Village to become a painter. I was just savvy enough to know the art world lay somewhere in that direction, not toward Paris. And I made sure that Rachel knew it, too.

But after a day of working for Lenny, my confidence vanished. I found myself holding on to only the barest wisps of that dream. To keep it from disappearing altogether, I told everyone I knew that I was going. I tested it out on the kids at school, gauging its plausibility by their reaction. They all thought it sounded great. I mentioned it to Lenny, who sighed deeply, then rolled his eyes, dismissing my dream as if it were vapor. But when I told my mother, she sensed, under my obstinate defiance, an aching need, and took me seriously.

She asked me to finish high school first, then apply to New York art schools if I liked. She was sure they'd have scholarships galore for a talented girl like me. She knew I'd skipped a lot of classes, that I couldn't graduate unless I attended summer school, but she thought my grades were passable. She had no idea what a mishmash I'd made of my education, and I was too ashamed to tell her. I always forged her spiky signature on my hopeless report cards.

I said I wouldn't even discuss attending summer school, a high school diploma was a sick joke, and as far as college was concerned, she didn't know anything. I was going to New York to the Art Students League and painters didn't fill out applications to go there. They just showed up.

I knew practically nothing, but my mother knew less. She begged me to speak to my art teacher and get his advice at least. I said I'd do it for her sake, when, in truth, I was more frightened by my plan than she was.

That Monday, I lingered after class until the other students left. Arnold was stacking drawing benches against the wall. I didn't broach the subject right off. I could barely speak to him without blushing.

I toyed with my kneaded eraser and asked if he'd ever been to New York City.

He looked at me quizzically. "I was born there."

I asked why he'd ever left and moved to this wasteland.

He laughed. "Bronchitis," he said.

I sat down on the model stand, folding a thonged foot under me, and told him I was moving there in June to find a garret in Greenwich Village and become a painter. Even as I said it, the idea sounded naïve and far-fetched. To make myself seem more worldly, I dropped names of New York artists I'd read about—Jackson Pollock, Andy Warhol, Salvador Dalí. I mentioned the Art Students League and asked if he had any tips.

"I'm afraid it had its heyday twenty years ago," he said. He quit stacking benches and offered me a cup of cold coffee. "You sure you want to do this? Aren't you a little young?"

I brushed off my youth as if it were fluff. I said I only brought up the Art Students League because so many famous people had gone there. I knew it was defunct. I was open to suggestions.

He thought for a moment, then rattled off a list of art schools I'd never heard of and had no idea how to apply to. He said he thought Cooper Union was free, or relatively inexpensive. He offhandedly mentioned that he traveled to New York a couple of times a year and would be sure to look me up and see how I was doing, buy me a hot meal if I needed one.

That cinched it—in fantasy at least. I had us meeting by assignation at the Waldorf-Astoria.

That winter, I worked for Lenny with a newfound rigor that stunned him. I even picked up odd jobs for Mrs. McCaffrey.

But I couldn't save. I wasn't wanton with my money. I didn't buy glitzy clothes or gadgets like my classmates did. I just felt the dire need to reward myself for all my dogged hard work, to splurge on the extra candy bar, the jumbo Coke.

Sometimes, when my friends complained about the travails of college-entrance requirements, a tinny rancor crept into my voice. It wasn't adult bitterness, the strident sneer of having been overlooked. It was more a breathless, childlike terror, the sense that I was being squashed before I started.

By spring, I'd barely saved four hundred dollars. I planned to leave anyway. I knew that if I didn't go soon, money or no money, common sense would overwhelm me and I'd never leave.

I started pricing one-way tickets to New York, charter prop planes that bumped down at La Guardia on their way to Europe. My mother begged me to reconsider, to put off going for another six months until I finished school and had saved more money. It was pointless. I'd never eke out enough credits to graduate. I'd squander whatever I earned. I was terrified to turn eighteen and still be working for Lenny.

I ignored my mother's pleas, and when she wouldn't let up, I rationalized and whined until I wore her down. She agreed to go with me to buy a duffel bag, then stood in aisle six of Woolworth, teary-eyed, as if we were picking out a coffin.

One afternoon, she told me that if I was really going through with it, she wanted me to see my father and say a proper good-bye. We both knew the real reason she wanted me to see him: My grandmother had recently passed away and she suspected my father had received a hefty inheritance. She hoped that if he saw me in person, he might remember he had a daughter and help me out.

The following evening, I drove down Van Nuys Boulevard to the Montego Arms. I cruised past its brown facade, as nondescript as a cardboard box, then parked on a side street. I didn't want my father to see my MG midget. It's not that I thought it made me look moneyed—it was roofless and dented. It's just that my dad couldn't grasp anything as impractical as my love for this dinky sports car, and I felt awkward enough as it was. We'd seen each other only three times in as many years.

I tapped on his door. I could hear the drone of a TV, the familiar shuffle of his imitation-leather Sears slippers.

He cracked open the door and peered suspiciously into the twilight.

"Hey, Dad, it's me, your daughter, Jill," I said. "I was in the neighborhood, so I thought I'd drop by."

He blinked rapidly, as much from befuddlement as from the dusky light. "Your mother mentioned you were coming."

"I'm here!" I said with forced levity.

"Do you want to come in?"

"Sure, Dad, that would be great."

"I've already eaten. I have nothing to offer you."

"I'm not hungry," I said. I stepped onto the cigarette-scarred green carpet. "So, did Mom tell you the big news?"

"She said you were going away."

"Yep, to the Big Apple."

He was wearing his old cotton bathrobe, knotted with a nylon kitchen cord. A pair of electric blue socks sagged around his white ankles. I noticed he had added a couple of house-plants—rubber and spider—to the Spartan decor. "You've fixed up the place. Looks nice," I said.

He grimaced, then waved his hands, shooing away my compliment as if it were a fly. "Oh, Jill, this is no way for a man to live."

I said I thought it looked okay. I sat down on the edge of his sofa bed, picked up a magazine, then set it down again. My father remained on his feet, nervously massaging his temples.

"So, Dad, have you ever been to New York City?" I asked.

133

My mother had coached me to keep the conversation on New York, then pick a warm moment to ask him for help.

"Your mother and I went there for our honeymoon. Oh, God, Jill, why did she do this to me?"

I stood up and walked over to the casement window. The pool had been drained of water, but the pool lamp was on. It looked like a saucer of incandescence in the concrete courtyard. "I guess we won't be seeing much of each other for a while," I said. It sounded ludicrous. My father and I never saw each other. I shut my eyes and took a deep breath. "Do you think you could help me out with the airfare, Dad?"

"I can't live like this anymore. I had a house. I had a garden. What happened?"

"I don't know," I lied. I started moving toward the door.

"You're leaving?"

"Yeah, Dad, with all the packing and everything—"

"Okay, okay. Take care of yourself, Jill."

I said, "You bet I will."

The stoplights on Van Nuys Boulevard were regulated by the police to curb drag racing, but every valley kid knew if you hit a steady forty, you could barrel through them. I gunned the accelerator.

———†———

I closed out my savings account. I bought a one-way ticket to La Guardia. I found a tiny trunk at Sears Roebuck in which to pack my art supplies and portable record player. (I still got my father's employee discount and I used it to the hilt.) I could only squeeze in three or four albums and I chose them with the

utmost care—*Sweet Baby James* for cathartic late-night lip synch-
ing sessions, *Clouds* because I thought the lyrics were profound,
and *Hair* to perk me up in case New York was not all I expected
it to be.

On my last night of art class, I dawdled in the hall until the
other students were finished. I heeled the wall and watched
them file out. As soon as they were gone, I slipped back into
the classroom and shut the door behind me. Arnold was leaning against a window frame, arms folded, eyes shut, yawning.
This time I approached him without a hint of coyness, without
the spark of a blush.

I unbuttoned the top three buttons of my peasant blouse,
crossed the ink-splattered floor, and kissed him.

He kissed me back, then stopped himself.

I had no precedent to go on except *Valley of the Dolls* and
Peyton Place. I asked him if he would sleep with me.

He looked stunned.

I mustered all my nerve and asked again.

"Maybe we should talk," he said.

I shook my head no.

"Sweetheart, I can't sleep with you. I'd like to, but I can't."

"I don't see why not," I said. I honestly didn't.

"For one thing, I could be arrested." He smiled, trying to
make light of things.

I had no sense of humor. "I won't tell anyone," I promised.

He put his hand on my cheek. He didn't caress me; he
simply pressed his hand against my skin. "It wouldn't be fair
to you."

The gesture felt so loving that I began to cry.

"Shhh," he said. He tried to take me around, but I kept my

135

face averted. As much as I wanted to be held, I was embarrassed to stain his shirt with my leaky mascara.

"I bet you think I'm a big jerk."

"It's the last thing I think."

"I've made such a fool of myself."

"No you haven't."

"Do you still like me?"

He cupped my head in his hands. I could tell he was choosing his words with great caution. "Jill, if you were older, I—"

"I'm old enough," I said flatly. At that moment, I felt unbearably old.

He gave me his handkerchief and I wiped up my wet, smudged red eyes. Then I handed it back to him, concealing the mascaraed mess in a jumble of folds. I walked over to the model stand and sat down, wrapping my arms around my knees. He sat down beside me and put his hand on my back. I could feel the heat of his palm through my blouse, the excruciating tenderness with which the pads of his fingertips rested on my neck.

"Will you still come see me in New York?" I asked. I didn't want to lose this. After all, I had nothing waiting for me there save vague plans and a fantasy.

"I'll try," he said.

"I guess I should go now."

"Jill, you don't have to leave right away. Would you like to get a cup of coffee and talk?"

I shook my head no.

"You sure?"

I nodded.

He insisted on walking me to my car and opened the

door for me. When I slid behind the wheel, he let his hand trace the breadth of my cheek, linger by my ear. I sank my face into his touch. Then I turned over the ignition and drove off, parking a couple of blocks away. I pressed my brow against the steering wheel, so embarrassed by what I'd done that the burn seemed to rise off my scalp. But I also felt a mad, thrilling power.

———†———

At the last minute, Mom insisted that Jack go with me to help me get settled. She borrowed a polyester winter coat from a neighbor (it had a white puff like a poodle tail topping its hood) and demanded I pack it. She had me change my measly savings, shrunk even more by the cost of the ticket, into guaranteed traveler's checks. She bought me two six-packs of cotton panties, a hairbrush, kneesocks, and a one-size-fits-all bra, then stuffed them into my duffel bag. She talked an old fling of hers in the used-car business into taking my MG on consignment when and if I needed money.

Lenny showed up the night before I left to give me two crisp one-hundred-dollar bills ("Don't blow them at Twenty-one, Jill") and the number of a friend of a friend with a crash pad where Jack and I could sleep the first night.

The whole family drove me to the airport. In the terminal, my teary mother didn't stop fidgeting with me—tucking my stubborn curls behind my ears, checking to see that I still had my ticket. I couldn't wait to get away. I kissed Tommy and Pete good-bye, hugged my mom, then hurried through the gate. Jack and I were flying on a charter plane that had exit signs marked in both Urdu and English. I squeezed into my seat while he tried to cram the bloated duffel bag under his. Through a pitted window no bigger than my own face, I could just see into the terminal. In a shocking-pink jumpsuit, my mom was easy to spot. She was covering her face with her hands, weeping in front of everyone, and it finally dawned on me that she wasn't crying out of motherly meddlesomeness, but for the genuine loss of me.

Then the plane took off.

PART

THREE

All during the long flight, I clung to the half-baked notion that I, above and beyond all others, would be spared life's wallops; that where others stumbled and quit, I'd catch myself and push on. By my estimation, I'd already paid my dues and life understood this and consequently would reward me, or at least, from here on in, dole out my fair share of its pleasures.

I also knew this was willed madness, but it was the last holdout I had of my youth and I couldn't give it up.

Jack and I splurged on a cab into Manhattan. It was dusk. Through the taxi's thick bulletproof divider, I could just make out the skyline. It looked like a false backdrop of steel and glass cut unevenly by a toenail scissors.

Having no idea where we were going, I asked the driver to take us to the "heart of Greenwich Village." I knew no other address. Jack and I had planned on calling Lenny's friend only as a last resort, as if, in the tiny sprocket of time between fading dusk and terrifying dark, a slew of other possibilities might crop up.

On a loud street corner that seemed to be the quintessential hub around which chaos swirled, Jack squeezed into a cracked glass phone booth and dialed hotels. We had a 1953 edition of *New York on $5 Dollars a Day* borrowed from an elderly neighbor. By the way Jack kept slamming down the receiver, I gathered things had changed since 1953.

Cars hurled down the avenue, thudding over potholes. Steam rose from manhole covers, taking on the shape of coloring-book clouds. The muggy air smelled as if a pilot light had gone out and gas was leaking. Every minute or so, a huffing blue bus hissed to a stop and spewed out throngs, from old women fumbling with lumpy bundles to skimpily clad teenagers decked out in love beads. They parted around my suitcase like rushing water breaking over a rock. I was terribly concerned that my record albums would get smashed. I straddled the Sears trunk, buffering it with my knees, and watched the last spokes of daylight roll down Sixth Avenue.

After a dozen tries, Jack climbed out of the booth and sat down beside me. He didn't say anything about where we'd spend the night, and I didn't ask.

Darkness dropped. A breeze hopped up. Refuse from a pizza stand, wax paper laden with grease and Styrofoam cups weightless as ions blew around our thonged feet. Having no idea what else to do, we called Lenny's friend. In a besotted ramble, the man said he couldn't put us up that night, but his niece, who also knew Lenny, probably could. She was looking for a new roommate anyhow. Terrified she'd turn us down and we'd have no place to go, I made Jack call her. After ten minutes in the booth (he didn't say more than two words), he hung up and shook his head as if to release an earful of water. He said he thought we were invited over but wasn't sure. The girl spoke so fast, he barely understood her. We hauled my duffel bag and record player into another cab and spent more of my savings barreling uptown. When the taxi jerked to a stop, we were in the East Fifties close enough to the river to smell the salt air. The streets were quieter here, dead-ended like valley cul-de-sacs and canopied with trees. Here and there, under flapping awnings, stood uniformed doorman. Yvette came down to her lobby in a pleated blue Catholic school tunic, black nail polish, and stiletto heels. She would have been ravishing if not for a doughy nose. She looked no older than I, but spoke in the husky whisper of a fifty-year-old lounge singer. She smoked unfiltered Chesterfields in a gold cigarette holder and referred to her father as Daddy Warbucks and her stepmother as Cruella Deville. She wanted to know all about me, but when I started to tell her, her eyes went out, poof, gone. She took us on a tour of her apartment, which turned out to be a single room with a low ceiling and a big brass bed in the center. She said she and I could share the bed, while Jack (she pointed at him as if he were a dog) could sleep on the floor.

As soon as the lights were doused, she asked me if I was sleepy. When I shook my head no, she lit a Chesterfield and started talking. She rarely took a breath and her voice formed a murmurous low loop of sound. In unbearable detail, she described all the dangers that could befall me in New York. She said she was only telling me this for my own good. She didn't use impersonal newspaper accounts, but real incidents from her own life: the time a well-dressed businessman cornered her in a subway and flashed a penis as long as a necktie, the law clerk of Daddy's who followed her home and tried to maul her in the lobby, the greengrocer who wanted to trade oranges for sex. And she gave me tips for basic survival.

"You can knee them in the balls, or gouge their eyes with your fingernails, or use any weapon you happen to have on hand, like a stiletto heel, to smash them in the windpipe. Then run."

Jack fell asleep, but I didn't. I fastened my mind around the rush of her words and hung on.

———†———

Yvette agreed to rent me my side of the bed for $87.50 a month. She hinted the place was worth twice that because of its tony location and her trifling price was an act of benevolence. After I forked over the money, I had only a couple of hundred dollars left, plus a smattering of change. Jack took me aside and urged me to get a job fast. He was staying only a week and he intended to see me settled before he left. He didn't stop badgering me.

Every morning, I hit the streets, intending to look for work, but I couldn't even get myself to buy the want ads, let alone inquire at employment agencies. Mostly, I wandered downtown, ambling along streets whose names were emblematic of overnight success—Broadway, Park Avenue, Forty-second Street. By the time I reached Greenwich Village, I almost expected to trip over opportunity, as if impulsive millionaire art collectors scoured St. Mark's Place looking for new arrivals.

In eye-frying colors and Indian beadwork, teenagers hunkered on every stoop. Or what passed for teenagers. The year was 1970 and hippiedom was in its heyday. I dressed like a hippie. I wore the obligatory bell-bottoms with frayed hems, the T-shirt little more than a rag. I even let my hair frizz out to the size of a medicine ball. But there was always the telltale sign that I worked for a living—the crease of a bra strap, a smudge of lipstick, a label that revealed I bought my clothes on sale at Sears.

Here, no one appeared to work. Eyes hooded and glazed, kids basked in sunlight or smoked reefer or languidly peddled skimpy rows of love beads slung from their wrists. Their idleness seduced me. I mistook it for bohemianism, which, by my reckoning, was the first stage an artist must pass through on her way to brilliance.

I squandered whole afternoons in their company.

From time to time, I wandered over to Cooper Union. The massive building, like the iron hull of a capsized tanker, stood wedged against a ceaseless barrage of traffic. Loitering outside, I scrutinized the art students, aching to ask one of them how to apply, but with no money, I was made mute by the sheer impossibility of my aspirations.

Around five, I returned to the apartment. Yvette was usually just waking up. She wasn't a hippie per se—*"Au contraire"*—but she didn't see the point of working for a living, and I admired her for that. I didn't see the point either.

Jack distrusted her. He thought there was something acutely wrong with her. Something "delusional" and "askew." Whenever he got me alone, he told me to find a job for Christ's sake and get the hell out of there. He reeled off Yvette's faults—nonstop talking, manic highs, weird sleeping hours. A long, petty list as far as I was concerned.

We fought. I said he came to these conclusions only because he viewed my new friend, my new life, through the pint-size lenses of the valley. He said I was acting like an immature child and that, as soon as he got home, he was telling Mom everything.

When he finally left for La Guardia, we barely hugged good-bye.

That weekend, my mother called. Her voice sounded nervous, with a ping of unadulterated panic. Knowing how touchy I could be, she mentioned only a couple of the incidents Jack had enumerated—my difficult job search, my new, dreamy attitude about work. Then, with dire restraint, she brought up Yvette and asked if what Jack had told her was true.

I sighed deeply. I said she knew perfectly well how strait-laced Jack was, how judgmental. The boy must have been a vicar in another life. She should have faith in my perception of people, a little trust in her own daughter. I said she had absolutely nothing to worry about.

———†———

My mother had everything to worry about. Yvette *was* crazy. Or on the iffy brink of it. Over the next few weeks, I watched her collect near-mortal fiascoes and hysterical encounters the way other people collect glass figurines or Fabergé eggs. She fought with every grocer for blocks around, with every neighbor who shared a common wall. She never returned from a cab ride without the driver having tried to rob or rape her. She rarely returned from a walk without a "perfectly respectable-looking" pervert having tried to flash her. She taped flesh-colored Band-Aids over her nipples, then wandered the streets in a loose-knit rope vest with see-through gaps the size of checkerboard squares. When men followed her, frothed for her, she screamed obscenities back at them. One day she came home breathless and announced with pride that a construction worker had toppled off a second-story scaffold while trying to ogle her. Another time, she greeted the Chinese delivery boy in only those Johnson & Johnson pasties, and when he gaped, she threatened to have him deported.

She wanted me to partake in her madness. She badgered me into wearing tank tops as thin as cheesecloth, short shorts as tight as Ace bandages. I mostly obeyed her; I didn't want her to find out I was a virgin. I had told her so many lies about myself, had matched every one of her lewd experiences with a made-up wanton encounter, that if she discovered the meager truth, I'd have shriveled up from shame. So I let her revamp me.

One afternoon, she had me dress to the nines—short skirt, slinky jersey, and platform shoes. She said she was taking me out to lunch, her treat. The restaurant she chose was near Wall Street, a garnet red room woolly with cigar smoke. We were the only women present. The maître d' whisked us across the floor, then stuck us in a corner. Yvette ordered for me, a dish I'd never tasted before. When lunch arrived, she leaned across the table and informed me, in a voice breathless with dervish giddiness, that she'd forgotten her purse and hadn't a dime on her. I froze, but she ate with relish. By the way she stared me down, I knew I had better eat, too. I chewed on my pressed duck and lentils as if they were cardboard and gruel. When the bill came, Yvette performed her big scene, all fluster and pouts

147

and crocodile tears until one of the men came to her rescue. Then, without so much as thanking him, she nudged me out the door, whispering, "I told you men were easy."

To keep up with her and stretch what was left of my savings, I walked dogs. No regular hours. I just showed up at the K-9 Club, picked up a fistful of leads and was paid in cash. I earned only a pittance, but I loved my charges—Lulu and Garth and Sadie and Tubs. Ears cocked, tails wagging, tugging me this way and that, they made me feel as if I were tethered to hope. When I described all my pups to Yvette like a besotted lover, she wanted to try walking dogs, too. She said I made it sound philosophical. Fool that I was, I took her along one morning and she got her own pack of dogs.

It was late summer. A slew of thunderstorms had just struck and the ground was still spongy. I took the lead while Yvette ambled behind. The dogs strained against their collars and splashed through puddles. One miniature dachshund, refusing to dampen its paws, had to be carried. Somewhere in Central Park, between a granite outcrop and a fake swollen lake, Yvette said, "This is so *boring*," then let go of her dogs and walked away. I watched as the spots and puffs and tails vanished into dripping foliage.

I returned my dogs, mumbling something about my roommate being slow today, and never went back.

After that, I hated her and I knew she didn't particularly like me. Probably never had. Since she hardly needed my piddling rent money (Daddy gave her a stipend), I couldn't figure out what my role in her life was. And then one night, I did.

The air conditioner had broken and Yvette, screaming through the crackling intercom for the "fucking super" to come fix it, lost patience, yanked open the window, and, without so much as glancing at the sidewalk below, nudged the unit into blue-black space. The thwack of the crash came up through my spine, made my teeth ring and my eyes water.

Yvette waited for me to calm down, then scrutinized my stunned reaction until it finally hit me.

The insane antics, ceaseless dramas, slam-bang fights, teasing sex shows only played well in front of an audience—a paying audience. I was the dupe who had bought the ticket.

As soon as my money was gone, so was I. But I made no preparations for my inevitable ousting. Instead, I sat on her bathroom floor and composed letters to Arnold.

Or tried to compose them. After the obligatory "How are you? Things here are great!" the pencil came to a skidding stop. I couldn't imagine what to put next. A recount of a rollicking New York party? Descriptions of museums I had yet to visit? A job I had yet to find?

I planned to lie to Arnold. It never occurred to me to do otherwise. But left unchecked, my teensy fibs invariably snowballed into runaway adventures Yvette might have had, and another day ended with me sprawled on the bathroom tiles, elbow-deep in half-written, pulverized letters. Only when, by sheer exhaustion, my lies turned humble and prostrated themselves before probability did I catch the swing of writing.

In modest, manageable language, I described the girl I was meant to be: a girl who trudged museums and attended art classes when she wasn't dog-tired from her part-time secretarial jobs. The anecdotes I invented about myself were so earnest . . . so, well, touching really, I actually felt I had lived them.

I made sure not to imply that I had it all licked though. I asked a number of urgent questions about New York so that Arnold would be forced to respond quickly. I knew it flattered men to be helpful.

Next, I bought a pocket dictionary (my first) and looked up word after word. Sometimes my attempts at spelling were so far off the mark that whole hours passed before I could find the right word and reshuffle *xhibite* into *exhibit*.

After everything was scratched out and corrected, I chose from my innumerable handwritings, a jaunty, slanted script, one that showed worldliness and discipline with a smidgen of girlish pride. When I reread the final results, I felt a kind of dazed charge that wouldn't return for years—the thrill of having created a truly fictional character.

Then I dropped the letter in a mailbox and waited for his response. Waiting became my full-time job, and would have been my chosen occupation if I hadn't run out of money.

Ten days after the rent was due, Yvette gave me two options—pay up or move out, *today*. For a second, I thought she was joking, but there was no leniency in her gaze—it was as hard and vacant as ever. I had thirty-seven dollars left. I acted all huffy and brave and pulled out my duffel bag. I flung my paltry array of cotton panties and one-size-fits-all bras onto the bed, then started packing. I gave deep, dramatic sighs, hoping to elicit pity where I sensed there was none. Yvette puffed on a Chesterfield and watched me. When I finished packing and zipped up my duffel bag, a jolt of cold panic burned in my throat, as if I'd just swallowed embers and ice.

"I can't believe you're doing this to me," I mumbled.

Yvette absently picked off a fleck of tobacco trapped in the corner of her mouth. "Why?"

"Because I thought we were friends."

She didn't even bother to respond.

I hauled my bags into the hall.

She stuck out her hand, palm up and platterlike. "The keys."

I gave her the keys. "You know I'm good for the money, Yvette."

"Really? I don't recall you looking for a job. Matter of fact, you've been hogging my bathroom for weeks, scribbling away at some letter. How were you planning on earning the rent? As a scribe?"

I closed my eyes. "Please," I said.

"Sorry, Jill. No can do."

Then she shut the door and I stood in the hall, slumped against the wallpaper. I couldn't think; my skull was a cave of wind. Finally, I joggled and bumped my suitcases downstairs and knocked on the super's door. In broken Spanish, I told his mother what had happened and asked if she could store my Sears trunk. I knew she hated Yvette even more than I did.

Next, I went to the nearest park, a smudge of grass on the river, and sat down on a bench. Trash barges floated by. Seagulls shrieked. I tried to conjure up a plan, even an inkling of a plan, but every idea flitted away in my howling head.

Wrapping my arms around my knees, I sat for so long, I

could feel the sunlight, like a warm tide, ebb over my skin. Around six, I returned to the apartment building. I buzzed and buzzed until Yvette allowed me back in.

"You have to let me spend one more night," I pleaded.

Even she must have sensed my terror; it crackled all around me. "Jesus Christ," she said. "One more night and that's it. Got it?"

I nodded, then, despite the ridiculous hour, put on my pajamas and climbed into bed. I lay as compressed as I could, careful not to take up more than a margin of mattress.

"This isn't negotiable, Jill. I'm not running a fucking charity for—"

"I heard you," I said.

But next morning, I still wouldn't leave. I asked if I could keep my mailbox key and she charged me a dollar for it.

She said she was going out for the day and, by the time she returned, she wanted me out of here, gone, vamoosed.

Then she trod to the door. I could hear the *rat-tat-tat* of her stiletto heels. "I mean it, Jill," she said.

I refused to look at her. I got up and went to the table. I moved so slowly, I might have been entrapped in aspic.

Do you ever have the sense you're occupying another's body? That the tilt of your head, a fist you make, the deliberate way you wet your lips are not your own, that they're pilfered from another's cache of gestures?

Pounding on the table, refusing to leave, bunching my lips as if I'd bitten into a sour fruit, I was my father.

For a moment, I squeezed my eyes shut, trying to obliterate the feeling. Then I got up and left. Hauling my duffel bag,

I drifted downtown. As frightened as I was, I didn't phone my mother. I didn't want to scare her.

There was a group of kids I'd gotten friendly with during my sojourns to the village. They hung out with the hippies, but, like me, they were only pseudohippies. Mostly, they were runaways.

One of the girls, Karen, lived in a squat near Avenue D. She had once invited me to crash at her place. I could see she suffered from loneliness. She'd moved to New York the same week as I had with ambitions even more preposterous than my own. She wanted to be a *Cosmopolitan* fashion model, then maybe skip up to Broadway. She was thin and pale with features so fair, they looked as if they'd been chalked on. She would have seemed nearly invisible if it hadn't been for her enormous breasts. They came at you like thrown footballs.

That afternoon, I found her at home. Or what passed for home—a tiny, moldy room in an abandoned apartment building. Other kids occupied other floors. She'd decorated her dank spot with found furniture and plastic flowers from Woolworth. She was just leaving for work and said I should make myself at home. Or, better yet, I could go with her. She knew I needed a job. Her boss was always looking for new girls.

I knew where she worked—Escapade Modeling Agency. Karen described the place as a natural stepping-stone to a big career in fashion, as if Oscar de la Renta swung by Escapade now and again, scouting for a pale girl in pasties.

The agency was in the Garment District, an enormous loft cordoned off into flimsy stages. Each stage was painted a different color to create "the unique Escapade mood"—the red

Valentine Room, the purple Versailles Room, the green Eden Room. I waited in the yellow waiting room (furnished not unlike a dentist's) while Karen went to fetch her boss. His name was Eddie and he looked like a man who had been pithed of desire.

He motioned me into his office and, without an inkling of inflection, asked me to undress.

"The pay?" I asked

"Fifteen bucks a half-hour session."

I said no thanks.

"Plus tips."

I undressed.

He walked all around me as though scrutinizing a car for scratches, then told me to stand at a three-quarter angle, bend one knee "seductively, kid," and push my hidden arm against my breast to make it appear larger.

Then he snapped a Polaroid to see if I was photogenic. He held the film up to a hot lightbulb and my image went through quick transformations—from ghostly wisp to sepia blur to stunned visage to full flesh tones.

Tacking it up on a cork bulletin board amid a row of others, he said I could start today.

Karen brought me a robe and took me to meet the other girls, eight lipsticked models not much older than I. They sat slouched in bathrobes on three mismatched sofas facing a poorly tuned black-and-white TV. A languid, petulant boredom permeated the room, as if they were all sisters grounded on a Saturday night.

Karen explained that the bulk of the job was spent waiting. "You wait for a 'photographer' to come in; then you wait for the jerk to choose you. The guys usually bring their own equipment, but if they don't, Eddie rents them a Polaroid and flash. He also sells film at outrageous prices. Some of the girls keep film in their pockets and, when Eddie's not looking, try to underbid him.

"Most of the photographers are just harmless losers who would probably faint if you touched them. But if some freak tries to grope you, you scream for Eddie. There's a strip of masking tape in front of each stage and it's a no-no for the men to cross it, but you can sometimes earn a big tip letting a guy take a sleazoid close-up."

A nondescript gray-haired man walked in, eyed us girls for a disconcertingly long time, and opted for Veronica. She seemed vaguely annoyed to be torn away from her TV show.

"The guys are obsessed with choosing the right girl for the right scenery. I guess that's the creative part. I'm always picked for the Valentine Room. They pretend to be all interested in the artsy-fartsy stuff like lighting and angle and mood. Then, like . . . da . . . it just dawned on them, they ask you to spread your legs a little wider.

"The trick is to get regulars. They tip the best and they're nicer, a lot nicer. Once in a blue moon, a real photographer drops in. Eddie told me that last year one of his girls got in *Penthouse*. She was the centerfold and everything. I mean, you never know," Karen said.

Around lunchtime, the place filled up, and I was finally chosen by a squat, bald man who looked like my old Beginning Business Machines teacher. I didn't want to be chosen, but you weren't paid if you weren't picked.

I followed him into the Versailles Room and sat down on

the red velveteen French Provincial sofa. A smidgen of foam eked out of its tulip-patterned cushions.

"What's your name, sweetheart?"

"Yvette."

"A Frenchy, huh? I was in gay ole Paree during the war." He bounced his hands in front of his chest as if he were shaking two huge jugs of milk. "Oo-la-la. Those French girls' titties were something else."

He studied me through the viewfinder. "Okay, sweetheart, slip off your robe and let's see what kind of knockers you've got."

I wasn't sure how to get the robe off without standing up, and I didn't think my knees would hold me. I yanked off one pink sleeve, then the other, and sat entangled in chiffon and velveteen.

He didn't seem to notice. He had honed in on my breasts. The flash kept popping.

"Rub them, sweetheart."

I pretended to wash myself.

"Harder, baby. Now squeeze them. Do you think you can lick your nipples for me?"

I said I wasn't that limber.

He ran out of film, reloaded the camera, and told me to stretch out on the sofa.

I struggled out of the tangled robe and lay down, facedown.

"Like that ass, sweetheart. Let me see more. Roll onto your back."

I rolled onto my back.

He bobbed and clicked.

"Spread your legs, darling, and show me some pussy."

I let my legs fall open no wider than an oblivious teeny-bopper wearing her first miniskirt.

"I haven't got all day, kid. Touch yourself."

I stroked my breasts again.

"Stop teasing me."

I put my hand on my thigh.

"Come on, sweetheart. You know exactly what I want."

He was right. I knew exactly what he wanted.

"Now come for me, baby. Give me a big scream."

I had climaxed in front of another person only once in my life—necking with a boy from the roller rink. We were at it for hours. He must have had his knee in the right place. I made the same face I wore that afternoon—one of astonishment and awe.

Then Eddie banged on the door, said time was up, and I got my fifteen bucks, plus a five-dollar tip.

———†———

Over the next few weeks, I slept at Karen's squat and worked for Eddie. On a good day, I made fifty dollars; on a bad, zilch. Eddie had a seniority system—the girls who performed fellatio on him got to pose on hopping Saturday nights. The rest of us got dead weekday afternoons. I felt lucky just to get a tip. Sometimes, while posing supine on a sofa, between the glaring lights and the men's scrutiny and my chilly nudity, I felt as if I were numb but conscious during my own operation. One night, without much thought, I picked up a college boy at a bar and got rid of my virginity with no more regret than you get rid of a dorky photograph of your younger self.

Whenever I could, I snuck into Yvette's building to check her mailbox to see if there was a letter from Arnold. I picked times of the day when I knew Yvette would be asleep, any hour before 3:00 P.M. I didn't want to run into her. I couldn't bear to hear her pampered, raspy voice snidely inquire how I was doing.

One morning, the super's mother stopped me. Along with my Sears trunk, she'd been holding my mail for me—a post-card from Rachel, a note from my mother, and a letter from Arnold. I tore it open in the park.

It wasn't at all what I'd expected. Arnold's tone was so . . . so teacherly. He had answered the letter of a girl who trudged museums and attended art classes when she wasn't dog-tired from her part-time secretarial jobs.

I barely recognized my own lies; I was no longer the girl who would even bother to make up such a girl.

I read his letter straight through. In a cautious but caring voice, he congratulated me on how well I was doing and gave me the names and phone numbers of people who could help me get even better jobs or just introduce me around the art world.

I skimmed the list of names. I couldn't bear to read them. The gap between what I'd become and these possibilities— "The Whitney Museum has an internship program"; "Phone Wooster Street Gallery and use my name"—seemed un-breachable.

Instead, I dwelled on the last paragraph. Just before Arnold signed off, there was a crack in his teacherly veneer. He said he thought about me a lot, a whole lot, maybe too much, and promised to call when he got to New York in late November or early December.

With utmost care, I folded and pocketed his letter, then read Rachel's postcard:

> Dear Kiddo, Berkeley's a trip. Have you read R. D. Laing? Try *The Politics of Experience*; it's amazing stuff! Yesterday, I went to my first antiwar march. I can't tell you how moved I was by all the protesters and their insistence on a better world. We're going to beat those bastards and end the war. Let me know how you're doing. Call collect!

I called her collect. On a break at Eddie's, I phoned her dormitory room and told her I had to speak fast, really fast, because the lunch rush was soon starting. In a voice revved by lack of sleep and homesickness, I described the men who took pictures of me, their oily stares and weird agendas. I described the way some of them gave you tips, how they held up a bill just beyond your reach, like a slice of ham above a trained dog, and made you snap for it. How you could almost feel the cold touch of their camera lens as it slid over your skin. How one of my regulars used his tripod, like an armature on which to mold his fantasies of me, and climaxed pressing himself against it.

I tried to make this last anecdote ring funny, but I couldn't get the right bite in my voice; I just sounded hopped-up and terrified.

Then I told her about the squat, its dankness and drafts, how the waning electricity was stolen from a streetlight, the rusty water from a hijacked pipe. I said I couldn't stay there much longer but that I had to find a way to hang on in New York until December.

Rachel was silent; she said she needed a couple of minutes to think.

"I haven't got a couple of minutes, Rachel. I have to go."

She wanted to know where she could reach me that evening, and when I said nowhere, she made me swear I'd phone her.

Around midnight, in a booth on the corner of Houston and D, I dialed her back. I didn't say much at first, just answered her queries with soundless shrugs, "how should I know's" and grunts. I felt ashamed I'd told her as much as I had.

Most of the booth's glass was gone and I couldn't blot out the hiss of traffic, the jangle of horns.

"Jill, do you have a pencil and paper on you?"

I didn't even bother to answer her.

"Okay. Just memorize this." She gave me her grandparents' address, a slew of numbers on Kings Highway. She said she'd just spoken to them in Coconut Grove, Florida.

"Rachel, I don't know what you're talking about."

"Just listen, for Christ's sakes. My grandparents said you can stay at their Brooklyn apartment. The super has the key. You just have to pay for utilities and heat. They are going to be gone all winter."

She gave me the address again and had me repeat it back to her. She insisted I move in the next day. Before hanging up, she made me promise I'd quit Eddie's, never go back.

"I promise," I lied.

In the morning, I left Karen a note, thanking her for her

hospitality. I folded it around a twenty-dollar bill. Then I packed my duffel bag and lugged it to the subway. I rode in the rear car, joggling out to Kings Highway.

The instant I stepped out of the station, I felt a tug of familiarity: The semiattached brick houses, the dairy delicatessen, the bakery window laden with corn-ryes plump as pillows and challahs thick as a giantess's braids evoked the Montreal of my childhood. Even the smell was the same, a mixture of gasoline and boiled cabbage.

I walked a half mile to Rachel's grandparents' apartment and had the super let me inside. The parlor was dark, cloistered behind thick burgundy drapes. When I snapped on the lights, hosts of tchotchke—jade ashtrays, pewter goblets, porcelain miniatures of Gainsborough's Blue Boy, a davening rabbi, a mustachioed English hunter and his spotted spaniel, a raja astride a smiling elephant—gleamed at me from every surface. It could have been my own grandmother's house.

I stretched out on the sofa and slept for fourteen hours.

From that point on, I modeled for Eddie only when I was low on cash. Mornings, I rode the subway into Manhattan along with the other working stiffs. Sometimes, however, halfway there, a jolt of panic overtook me and I bolted through the hissing doors, rushed across the platform, and rode back. If I was flush, I bought kreplach soup at the corner deli, then ate it in front of Rachel's grandparents' television. I was careful not to spill a droplet.

One afternoon at Eddie's, I let a customer cross the scuffed masking-tape line to take as many close-ups of me as he wanted to. Then, using his generous tip, I retrieved my Sears trunk and hauled it back to Brooklyn in a cab.

I could barely lug it up the steps. The handle had broken. The trunk felt as if it had gained weight during the dormant weeks. Dragging it into the parlor, I set it by the sofa and pried open its stubborn lid. I couldn't believe what I'd brought to New York—india ink, pen points, Conté crayons, watercolor pads, minicanvases. I brushed aside the untouched art supplies and hoisted out my record player. Then I dug out my albums— *Clouds, Hair,* and *Sweet Baby James.*

For some reason, I couldn't listen to *Hair* or *Clouds,* but I played *Sweet Baby James* over and over and over again—for hours on end. Facing the pink-cheeked Blue Boy, the davening rabbi, and the smiling elephant, I lip-synched my heart out.

I sang about abject loneliness and pitch-black prairies, about bad weather and nervous breakdowns.

Though no more than an occasional groan escaped from my throat, I made all the right faces. I shut my eyes and opened my mouth in a baleful grimace. I took no more breaths than James Taylor did until the cords of my neck grew stiff and strained. I almost hyperventilated from lack of oxygen and the dizzying sense of my own isolation.

One day, I stopped going into the city. Then I stopped leaving the apartment altogether. The corner deli delivered, and for the next week or so, I lived on french fries, Mars bars, cream sodas, and chicken soup. Sometimes whole days passed without me talking to another soul but the delivery boy. And he didn't speak English. One night, I even quit lip-synching. Whenever I opened my mouth, it felt as if my soul were rattling in my chest like a dried-up kernel. Finally, I couldn't take it any longer and phoned my mother to see if she had enough money to send me the airfare home.

I said she could sell my MG if she needed to.

My mother had no idea what I had been up to. (I'd been calling her once a week from various pay phones, making up one cockamamy lie after another.) Though I assured her I was hunky-dory, just tired of the New York art scene, she could hear the frenetic pitch in my voice, the spacy pauses.

She told me I'd have the money by week's end, even if she had to rob a bank.

After I hung up, I curled up on the sofa, burrowing my face in the cushions. I felt awful about the fiasco I'd made of my future, about not being in New York when Arnold finally arrived, but I justified my bailing out. After all, I wasn't making art and I couldn't very well seduce Arnold on Rachel's grandmother's flowered sofa with Blue Boy and the davening rabbi looking on.

When my mother spied me amid the arriving airline passengers, I saw her look of distress. I was jittery and wan, clutching my scuffed trunk and bedraggled bag as if they were orphans. She hugged and kissed me, then cupped my thin face in her palms and pecked me on my unruly eyebrows. Hoisting up my luggage, she cautiously asked about my New York "trip," "vacation," "experiment," but when I grew irate and mute, she knew enough to quit. On the drive home, just to break the awful silence, she tried to catch me up on valley gossip, but I let her patter slide by with the billboards.

When we pulled up to the house, my MG midget was waiting for me. With unabashed pride, she said she didn't need to sell it.

I shot it a perfunctory glance, hugged my three brothers, then went—no, took—to bed. For the next three weeks, I rarely got up. My mother indulged me, keeping workaday life away from my bedroom door. Anything and everything—a

164

phone message from Rachel, the whir of the garbage disposal, padding across the pink-flecked bathroom linoleum—seemed hallucinatory in its familiarity. Sometimes, the simple pattern of my bedspread—apple plum orange, apple plum orange—caused me to cry. If I thought about Arnold and how I'd wrecked my chance with him by leaving New York too soon, I became despondent, almost bereaved. When my brothers spoke to me, it sounded as if they were talking through pressed cardboard and water.

Every day, I slept until noon, then scuffed over to the TV to watch a rerun of *Ben Casey*. In stark black and white, the opening credits immediately calmed me. A gaunt, elderly doctor with a corona of white hair chalked the basic symbols of life on a blackboard—man, woman, birth, death, and infinity. His hand was so ancient, it looked like the hand of God. The rest of the show—the car crash and cancer victims, the woman with tic douloureux whose face twitched like a glitch on the screen, the little boy with aplastic anemia who had to live in a Saran Wrap bubble—seemed almost beside the point. When *Ben Casey* was over, I got dressed and drove eight miles to the Bagel Factory to buy one sesame seed bagel. It had to be sesame seed. The thought of onion, or poppy, or garlic caused me to lose my appetite. If the factory had sold out of sesame that day, I simply didn't eat lunch. Then I drove home, slipped back into bed and read Mary Renault novels about ancient Greece. My concentration was almost nil, but I could still hang on to images of bronzed gods, Oedipus slaying his father, and sacrificial virgins. By early afternoon, a jittery exhaustion overtook me again and the pages blurred, cartwheeling away into visions. One afternoon, I saw a young Ben Casey, stripped to the waist—hairy, sweating—brandishing a sword before a bound, weeping me. Then a forgotten sesame seed slipped out from between two molars and its taste was so comforting, it helped edge me back into oblivion.

———†———

Perhaps it was the Greek idea of destiny, or Ben Casey's pill-size epiphanies, or my mother sending away in my name for trade school brochures (the pasteup artist, "see if you can draw Dinky the Duck" variety), or maybe I just became tired of my own despondency, but one day I couldn't stand it any longer. . . .

I went to my old high school library to look up local art colleges. Just to take a gander at the possibilities. Beside the checkout desk, on a steel gray shelf labeled YOU AND YOUR FUTURE, stood a thin stack of college catalogs. I plucked out any that had the word *Art* on the spine. The first one showed snaps of Annette Funicello and Frankie Avalon–type teenagers drawing from bikini-clad models. Another showed examples of student paintings—acidhead renditions of a Norman Rockwell–like family, Hallmark versions of a Salvador Dalí landscape. Only one catalog was devoid of psychedelic drawings and cookie-cutter sculptures. It even hinted at prophecy. Comparing itself with the Bauhaus and Black Mountain College, it talked about the "death of painting" and the avant-garde. (Whenever I saw the word *avant-garde,* I pictured ranks of young artists in black turtlenecks, pale but determined, marching into the future.) The college was called Cal Arts, and it had just enough snob appeal to intrigue me. I felt I had a certain

New York sophistication now. I slipped the catalog under my T-shirt and took it home.

I read it innumerable times, pondering the enigmatic questions it raised: "Aren't you an artist the day you decide to be one?" "How many life-drawing classes must an artist take to make an earthwork in the desert?" I practically memorized its courses: Happenings, Multimedia Workshop, Conceptual Art. Whenever I came to the admission requirements, however, I felt as if I'd been thwacked in the chest by a sucker punch. The college asked to see my high school transcripts and expected me to take the Scholastic Aptitude Test.

I slunk back to bed, but the numbing solitude, the unnerving idleness (after all, my days pitched and troughed by a TV show) were insufferable now.

One morning, I called up the college and asked to speak to the Admissions Office. I crushed the phone against my ear and waited out the ceaseless hum of being abandoned on hold. I wanted in so badly, it almost felt like a fever. When a voice finally came on, I bragged about my nonexistent portfolio, then made up some cockamamy story about misplaced transcripts, constant moving, and, inspired by a *Ben Casey* episode, whole semesters lost to childhood asthma. I even dropped hints about private tutoring in New York. The Admissions officer, a spacey, snobbish woman who took the longest drags on cigarettes I'd ever heard, said if my portfolio was as good as I claimed it was, the college might accept an exceptionally high SAT in lieu of high school grades.

I thanked her profusely. I got the general drift. The instant I hung up, however, just to be sure, I dug out my pocket dictionary and looked up *lieu.*

Despite a lingering sense of despondency, I put myself on a boot-camp schedule—up early, sketching till ten, then running through a gauntlet of charcoal exercises. Afternoons, to prepare my portfolio, I hauled out bookcase-size canvases and wrestled with pigments. I painted expressionist nudes à la de Kooning with checkerboard backgrounds à la Mondrian. Sometimes, I felt so abysmal about the results, I had to hold my squirming being in a hammerlock until the paintings worked on their own.

One day, the SAT forms arrived in the mail. They included sample questions I couldn't make hide nor hair of. The geometry diagrams looked like unchartered constellations, the algebraic formulas like gibberish. One question asked me to sort through a shelf of textbooks—If *Biology* is left of *Anatomy,* and *Anatomy* is stacked beside *Zoology* but not touching *Physics,* then where would we find *Astronomy?* I concentrated, shuffling and reshuffling these phantom books until their pages pulverized in my mind.

I flopped down on my bed and squeezed my eyes shut. By the racket my pulse made banging in my ears, I thought my heart would blot me out. I drew up my knees, tucked my hands between my thighs, and willed myself into unconsciousness.

When I awoke, as though fear had sobered me with a splash of cold clarity, I knew exactly what to do. Had probably known what to do from the moment I sent away for those forms.

I took out the SAT application and scrutinized it, front and back. The top half was bracketed with teeny squares into which one squeezed one's name, address, birthday, and sex. Any penmanship would do for that part. Toward the bottom, however, were a couple of blank spaces to be filled out by the applicant. The names and addresses of all the schools to whom test results were to be sent. That section would take some work. And, of course, there was the obligatory signature line.

I dug out an old letter of Rachel's and studied her handwriting. She had what I called the up-and-coming script—all the letters slanted in the right direction. It was a script I intended to emulate.

Next, I chose a slightly blunt pencil, one whose point wouldn't crack from the pressure. I didn't want any mishaps or erasures. Besides, the duller the point, the less specific the line.

Finally, I held the pencil with Rachel's confident grasp, jotted down the college to which my scores were to be sent, then signed my name in meticulous pushes and pulls, as I imagined she would sign it. If anyone grew suspicious later on, I wanted every detail right from the start.

I slid the completed form into its preaddressed envelope, sealed it with a lick, then drove down the hill and mailed it.

I figured Rachel would be horrified by my plan, see it as another one of my moral slippages, so I got my story straight before I called her. She wanted to help the poor; I was bust. She wanted to topple the hierarchy; I was as good a kingpin as any. I'd make me her civic duty. I knew she fancied herself as a cross between a Maoist and a revamped Florence Nightingale. I intended to appeal to the candy striper within the revolutionary.

To my astonishment, she thought her taking the test for me

was a terrific idea. Said her poli-sci prof had discussed the biases inherent in such exams, how they nudged out the hoi polloi and pandered to the privileged. While she read me statistics, I squashed my brow against the wall and prayed that all her trips to Europe, all her French lessons hadn't been wasted, that she'd do really, really well on *my* tests, and that by proxy, instead of being thrown a couple of chocolates from the bountiful plate she scorned, I'd finally get asked to the table.

———†———

Once I felt I had a toehold on hope, I submitted my portfolio, then went to see Arnold. I didn't call him beforehand. I couldn't fathom what we would say. I counted on the brash physicality of my youth to shore up any slump in the conversation—I'd learned that much at Escapade.

Arnold's studio door was unlocked. I gave it a sham knock, a brush of knuckles, then stepped inside. He lay on his cot, asleep in a puddle of lamplight. His heavy square eyeglasses, pushed back on his forehead, doubled the lamp's glowing filament in miniature, like two magnifying glasses collapsing the sun to start pinpoints of fire.

I shut the door behind me and slid the stubborn bolt into its rusty lock. Then I crossed the studio and stood over him. A book lay open on his chest; his arm dangled over the cot. A faint dusting of black hair silhouetted his forearm. He stirred, squinted up at me, and started to speak. I hushed him, touching his dry lips with my fingertips. Then I peeled off my ribbed T-shirt, lingered for a wooden moment in full lamplight, and lay down beside him. It wasn't hard to seduce him. The suggestion had already been implanted. My previous attempt, clumsy as it had been, must have tugged on his imagination until it unleashed tendrils of fantasies.

I tried to do everything adroitly—stroke suavely, lash my tongue with his. I had picked up a few moves. I gave a fair impression of a lover. I made all the right faces, astonished when a groan escaped from my throat, not unlike the unrehearsed moans that slipped out during lip-synching.

What I craved was elementary: that the exquisite pressure of his hand on my skin would somehow shape the amorphous being that I was into someone whole.

I laid my head on his chest afterward and prayed that we wouldn't have to make small talk. I'd never planned past this moment—all fantasies broke off here. On the far side of his chest lay an abyss.

I watched as swatches of light skidded across his studio ceiling. The sun was setting. All that remained of the afternoon were a few mauve streaks of smog.

"Jill," he said, cupping my face in his hands, "I have to get up, sweetheart. I'm supposed to be somewhere."

I stiffened.

"Jill, I didn't know you were coming over. Had I known, I—"

I said, "Hey, it's no problem." I said, "Hey, I have to be somewhere, too."

Then I made up an inane, labyrinthine lie involving a rendezvous at a bar, meeting some friends at a restaurant, a movie for which I already had tickets. I even blathered out the plot of the movie.

He held me while I talked myself dry.

When I finally shut down, I pressed my face into the hollow of his arm and took in a deep whiff of him, trying to glut myself with the intimacy of his smell. I couldn't bear to leave him just yet. I said, "I probably should have called first, huh?"

He laughed. "No, you made quite an impressive entrance."

I got up and started groping for my jeans, but he drew me back for another kiss and asked if he could see me again.

I said, "Of course."

Then, slipping on his heavy square eyeglasses, he watched me get dressed. Escapade had taught me only the craft of undressing. I drew up one foot, swaying like a jonquil in the wind, then yanked on my tangle of denim and tie-dye. Propping himself up on his elbow, he asked how long I was going to be in town.

"Eternity," I said. "I've pretty much had it with the hubbub of New York."

He looked at me quizzically. "I assumed from your letter that you loved New—"

"I got a tad carried away in my letter."

He smiled and asked where I was living.

"With my mom."

That sobered him. He got dressed, too. Then, gracing the nape of my neck with his fingertips, he walked me to my car, discreetly shot a glance around the parking lot, and kissed me good-bye.

I sped home, ignored my family, lined up like crows in front of the TV, and slipped into my room. I stretched out on the bed and pressed my palms against my eyelids. Then, with hallucinatory intensity, so that every gesture, every turn of his head left a phosphorescent trace, I replayed the afternoon.

By my estimation, it was Arnold's call now. I fully expected him to court me, woo me. The fact that he was three decades older, married, and had children seemed beside the point. I had declared my love; I thought I'd made myself perfectly clear.

My understanding of ardor was borrowed from books and their big-screen versions: Laurence Olivier, all rain-whipped and ravishing, bellowing for Cathy on the moors; Clark Gable's lips gracing Vivian Leigh's white throat. When I watched Zeffirelli's pastel-tinted *Romeo and Juliet*, I saw perfect love, not intricate social tragedy.

Adrift on my bed, I envisioned my love in Shakespearean proportions, when in truth, my fierce yearning, with its dogged single-mindedness, was closer to White Fang's unwavering love for "the man" than to Elizabethan courtship.

When Arnold failed to call me after three weeks, I sank into a state of despair that made the other one look like a feeble preliminary. I couldn't sleep. I lost my appetite. Even sesame bagels tasted like grit and sawdust.

Each time the phone rang, even after a month, the trill bore through my being. One evening, Rachel called to tell me she'd just aced my SATs. (Clutching the receiver, I was so discombobulated, I'd actually forgotten she'd taken them.) Her voice, all breathy with excitement, should have made me weep with gratitude for a friend who was always there for me. It didn't. I barely responded.

Next morning, I looked up Arnold's home address. I wasn't planning to park outside his house. I wasn't one of those rejected mad women who lurk in their lover's shrubbery. Though I considered it. Instead, I plotted the various routes he might take from his house to his studio. Then I drove them relentlessly. I figured if we just casually ran into each other, idled side by side at a stoplight, he'd glance my way and realize what he was missing. At seventeen, I understood cruelty, indifference, obtuseness, that life wasn't divvied up fairly, but I couldn't fathom unrequited love. Arnold drove a cream-colored Volkswagen, a popular car in those days, and when I scanned my windshield, the entire world consisted of white Volkswagens or runny blurs.

Just when I thought longing would derange me, I received a letter from him, typed and formatted in the semiblock style that Mrs. Hull, my old typing teacher, had taught us for a less formal business tone. And short. A little too short.

> Dear Jill,
> Are you <u>ever</u> coming back to class? Please call.
> > All the best,
> > Arnold

I sat down beside the mailbox and read the letter obsessively. I was too stunned to take it in. I needed to find some word or phrase or mark—the thick underline, say—to crack its meaning. I honestly didn't know whether his letter was a hint that I should call him or if he just wanted me to return to class, be his mere student again, and this wounded me unspeakably. I couldn't conceive that he might be wary of writing an open and frank letter about our sexual tryst—our budding love affair, by my estimation—then mailing it to my mother's house. Couldn't imagine what his hesitation might be.

Besides, I'd already told my mother I slept with him, was in love with him. She wasn't thrilled by the idea and said as much. But she said it in the soft, consoling tone mothers use to cushion their children's wildly careening dreams.

We fought. I intended to see him again. I was beyond reason. I had the granite-solid determination of inexperience on my side, and she was spent, plumb tired. (I think she also harbored a teeny hope that an affair with an older man might tame me.)

And really, what could she say? Of the two men she was dating, one was married, and the other was fifteen years younger than she and also named Arnold.

When Arnold phoned a couple of days later, on the guise of a follow-up to his letter, he kept up the ruse until he realized it was me on the line, then wanted to know when he could see me.

I sped to his studio. (I still didn't understand the reason for all the subterfuge.) The fact that he had a wife and kids—even the concept of wife and kids—was unreal to me, a disposable black-and-white, two-dimensional family that came with every dime-store picture frame.

I opened his door without knocking. He was sitting on his cot wearing a fresh white T-shirt. His khakis, socks, and shoes still held a splattering of the day's paint, as if they'd been cut from a single bolt of smears. I acted all casual, glancing at the unfinished canvas. I did the squint, take a step backward, cock the head routine I'd seen in galleries. But when he stood up and put his arms around me, I started to cry. I tried to turn away, but he held me against him. "What is it?" he asked. "What's wrong?"

I pressed my brow against the eye-frying white of his T-shirt. I said, "I didn't think you were ever going to call."

"Jill, I felt preposterous phoning your mother's house. I—" He cupped my head in his hands. "I didn't know if you wanted me to. Why didn't you call me?"

I said I'd already used up my quotient of bravery just showing up at his studio in the first place.

For a couple of minutes, I just stood there, letting my head be cradled in his hands. Then Arnold touched my breast through my macramé vest. He didn't caress it; he simply pressed his hand against me and we lay down on the narrow cot and made love.

When we parted this time, I made sure we had a foolproof game plan for getting back together. Since Arnold was wary of calling my house, I suggested he use another name if someone else answered the phone—Sheldon, for instance.

Then I told my family that Arnold would be calling as Sheldon and they had better not forget to give me the message.

Even my mother had to laugh.

I couldn't stay away from him. Each time he called, I chucked aside whatever I was doing and let the day's errands flit away in skewed orbits. I, who had no sense of time, arrived on time, then lay by his side, head on chest, with canine contentment.

For the first month or so, he tried to keep me at—if not arm's length—wrist's length. He intimated there was something I didn't grasp, a demise, an inevitable end, a sorrow I couldn't imagine. He kept saying he didn't want to hurt me, that that was the last thing in the world he wanted, and that maybe we should stop seeing each other. I knew he was as besotted as I. His worries struck me as preposterous. I insisted I had everything under control. Hey, at seventeen, I wasn't looking to get married. But the nanosecond after I left him each time, I felt breathless, almost panicked from a sense of longing.

———†———

One night I came home from Arnold's to find a letter on my pillow. The return address was Cal Arts. My mother had propped it there. I knew that because she'd already opened it, nudged the flap free with a butter knife, then resealed it with Elmer's glue. I could smell the tart adhesive. I turned on my pogo-stick pole lamp and sat down in the bright islands of light. Then, as if opening an unknown package—letter bomb or sweepstake prize—I rebroke the seal.

It took me a halting minute to absorb it. With great pleasure, the provost welcomed me to the college. He congratulated me on my portfolio, then, without mincing words, broke through the official protocol to say he'd personally made an exception in my case and skirted the high school diploma requirement. Evidently, my SAT scores had been astronomical. I was awarded a scholarship, not the whole kit and caboodle, but enough to give me a running start.

I could hear my mother stirring through the wall. I went into her room, letter in hand, and perched beside her on the bed. Neither of us bothered to pretend she hadn't read it already.

"Pretty incredible, huh?" I said.

"Who took the test for you?"

"Thanks for the vote of confidence, Mom. What makes you think I didn't take it?"

She gave a deep sigh.

"Rachel," I said at length.

She shook her head, trying to don a look of disapproval, but I could see giddiness cracking through. "It's just one test, I guess."

"And I came up with the idea that Rachel take it. I mean, that bodes well for my brilliance. I could have had one of the Kerkorian sisters take it."

She laughed. "It is pretty incredible. You did paint the portfolio, didn't you?"

"I can't believe you even said that."

She picked at a ragged fingernail. "How much money do you think you'll need?"

I figured a couple of grand.

She started gnawing on the nail. "We could always ask your father." She said it as a bitter joke; when Jack started college the year before, my father had tried to use it as an excuse to jettison Jack from his medical plan.

"I'll try to help, Jilly, but—"

I said I knew she had no money.

"I suppose you could always work for Lenny again. And what about those gals from Chicago. Didn't you do a perfume survey for them?"

I said I'd skip the Chicago gals and start with Lenny.

"Alas, she deigns to call me," Lenny said after I spelled out my situation. "You know, things aren't what they used to be. These are paranoiac times, Jilly Beans. My clients are checking every niggling survey, and I must say, doing things legit has certainly cut down on profits. A girl with your specialized talents is becoming a relic."

"I just need a job, Lenny."

"Most of the work's out of town. These are no-frill jobs."

I said I didn't care.

"Seattle. Three weeks, starting next Monday."

I didn't want to go. I didn't want to leave Arnold for that long.

"Yes or no, kid."

I said, "I'll do it."

I left for Seattle that Monday. Lenny gave me a piddling per diem and put me up at the YWCA. It was no Ramada Inn. I lived in a cell-size cubicle—steel cot, steel bureau, gray blanket, plastic crucifix. The closest thing to remote control TV was leaving the window cracked and watching the breeze turn the pages of the Gideon's Bible.

The Y was packed with girls from the Deep South, bussed to Seattle to participate in a spanking-new government vocational-training program. They were studying to be seamstresses, cashiers, and, in some cases, hotel maids.

When I could penetrate their thick, syrupy drawls, I enjoyed their company, and I believe they enjoyed mine, admired my irreverent, mile-a-minute goofball patter. When I told them I was from New York City, they claimed to have never met a "Nu Yuk Ju'ess 'fore."

I think they also liked me because I took an interest in their lives—a pathological interest. These were girls with scant opportunities. The dinky hamlets they were being bussed back to had no factories, let alone hotels in which a white-aproned maid dusted. They knew they'd never land a job when they were through with their training, any more than they'd marry the pink-cheeked naval cadets they necked with in the park. They figured six weeks in Seattle was the only vacation they'd ever get.

I told them flat out it didn't have to be so; they could go to college like me. After all, I was a high school dropout, too. I failed to mention I'd snuck into my rosy future by falsifying my exams. I failed to mention it because I no longer believed I had. Didn't I paint the portfolio that won me entrance? So what if I didn't take one lousy test. Rachel may have held the corporeal pencil during the corporeal exam, but she only acted as a medium through which my shrewd street smarts, my native talent, shined. But late at night, alone in my cell, I had serious doubts about my abilities and I needed these hard-luck girls to weigh myself against.

When they showed me snapshots of their betrothed, Joe Bob and Gary Lee, rail-thin boys with farmer tans, I told them all about my Arnold, how he was a famous artist. I didn't mention his wife. Some of the girls were deeply religious.

They attended church every week. One Sunday, they invited me to go with them. (Sundays were intolerably lonely for me—no work, couldn't call Arnold because he was home with his family, couldn't spend a dime because I was scrimping for school, couldn't even mosey around downtown because Seattle was all soup, drizzle, and gusts.) So I went.

I explained to the girls that I didn't believe. Quite the contrary. The story of Jesus—spermless conception, water into wine, a resurrection despite—*what?*—a two-ton stone blocking the grave!—struck me as no more plausible than a UFO sighting. Less. I sometimes believed in UFOs.

But I thought, Once I'm going to church, I might as well put the time to good use just in case 20 billion people aren't wrong.

While my friends got down on their knees (carefully, so as not to run their nylons), I rummaged through my memory for old school prayers and coupled together a vague medley, interspersed with a chorus of earthly desires. "Our Father, who art in Heaven, hallowed be thy name, please let me succeed at something, dear God, and give us this day this something bread, and forgive us for trespassing as we walk through the valley of the shadow of death. . . ."

When I ran out of prayers, I started in on religious maxims gleaned from old movies like *Ben-Hur* and *The Ten Commandments.* "And God said, Let there be light. An eye for an eye, a tooth for a tooth. Father, forgive them; for they know not what they do."

The girls rose and kneeled, rose and kneeled beside me. I could smell their cheap perfume. These were tough girls— one had been a prostitute; two had been to jail—but they were guileless in their belief. They wore the same gobbed-on makeup that I once wore—coal black eyeliner, mint green eye shadow, hair ratted into cumulus clouds. And I knew the only thing that truly separated us, cleaved our futures, was unadulterated luck and my willingness to cheat, and I intoned the only biblical snippet that made any sense to me. I said it with piety and true heart, "There but for the grace of God go I."

The day after I got back from Seattle, I was coming out of the supermarket, juggling a tub of ice cream, when, for the life of me, I couldn't remember where I'd parked my MG. I thought I'd left it by the Dumpster, bumper-to-radial with a souped-up Chevy, but a red Dodge sat in its place. I hurried up to the Dodge, half-expecting it to transmogrify into the squat shape of my beloved car.

Two florid-faced children sat hunkered in the rear seat, cheeks swollen with jawbreakers, staring up at me through the steamy window.

I started combing the parking lot. It was high noon. The ice cream began liquefying in my arms.

I was in Panorama City, ground zero, the bowl of the valley. Smog, grime, smoke, and diesel haze all sifted down through LA's gummed-up stratosphere to accumulate here. Just to glance across the street, buzzing with traffic, scorched your eyes. I chucked away my sloshing ice cream and tried to calm myself, figuring maybe I was just discombobulated and had missed the car on the first go-round.

I started trudging the hot asphalt again, squinting down rows of hoods. After a half hour or so, it finally sank in that my MG had been stolen. Hoping for a clue, I rushed back to the spot near the Dumpster, but all I found were rubber tread marks, like smudged chicken scratches, embedded in the pavement. They could have belonged to any car.

I sat down on a cement log and tried to catch my breath. It felt as if I'd been struck in the chest by a tire iron. I had no insurance, and without insurance, I couldn't replace my car, and without a car, I couldn't work, and without work, I couldn't afford art school, and without art school, I'd never make the lunge of faith to become a painter, and without painting, I'd wind up a lost, soulless woman working the lunch counter at Woolworth, and Arnold would never leave his wife for me.

By the time I called Jack, I was in a state of mourning. He picked me up and drove me to the police station. The desk sergeant, a man who Brylcreemed his flattop, tried to hurry me through the theft report. When I gave him detailed descriptions of my MG—"The dent in the passenger door looks like a crumpled bird's wing; the color is lipstick red"—he jotted down, *ding, door, red.* You could tell he didn't want to hear my troubles. To him, white trash lose cars like other citizens lose umbrellas.

In a last-ditch effort, Jack and I cruised the neighborhood just in case some kids had abandoned the car after a quick joyride. We started in Panorama City and moved out in concentric circles, crawling along cul-de-sacs where fourplexes stood cloistered behind aluminum-foiled windows, each reflecting a thousand suns in the foil's crumpled surface. The only cars we came across were clunkers or low-riders.

I said it was hopeless. I said my car could be a hundred miles away by now. I wanted to quit.

Jack insisted on another sweep.

"Please, Jack, I just want to go home."

"Trust me, Jill. You don't want to go home."

"And why not?"

"Because Dad's there."

"Very funny," I said.

"I'm not joking. The old man's been coming around lately."

"What the hell does he want?"

"I think he's lonely."

"I can't believe this," I said. "What the fuck does Mom do?"

"Disappears at the first sign of his Pinto. When you were in Seattle, she actually scaled the neighbor's fence and took the kids with her."

I squashed my fist against the windshield and scanned another cul-de-sac—Falcon, Impala, Mustang, Fury.

"It no big deal, Jill. I stay in my room. He's sort of mellowed."

"I knew we should have changed the locks."

"Really, he just sits around reading the stock report or staring at nothing. He says he's waiting to see the kids, but I think he really wants to see Mom. This is the bizarre part—sometimes, if no one's around, he goes out back and gardens."

———†———

My father was sitting at the kitchen table when Jack and I got home. He didn't look up. I'm not sure he even heard us. He was wearing an electric blue shirt with matching blue pants, a real shocker. The cobalt practically crackled off his sleeves. Jack hugged me, promising to look for my car again whenever I wanted him to, then slipped into his room. I loitered in the foyer, not sure what to do.

Several months before, in a manic spurt of redecorating, my mother had bought Wild West saloon doors for the kitchen. They were made out of cheap chipboard and flung thunderously open at a mere touch.

I didn't mean to make such a racket.

My dad reeled around, blinking and bewildered. He was larger than I remembered. And heftier. And the combination of his weight, and presence, and the electric blue shirt with matching blue pants made him look frighteningly permanent, like something massive and upholstered.

He gave a stiff shake of his head, then looked at me with blurry recognition. "Jill? Oh, Jill, I haven't seen you in . . . in—"

"Since before I went to New York," I said.

"Did you have a good time?"

"A regular ball, Dad."

I opened the fridge and poured myself a glass of Tang, trying to ignore him. But I could see he wanted to talk. I could sense his abject loneliness. My dad had no social armor, not even a hilt to parry his steely daughter; his needs were open and raw. I gave in and poured him a glass, too.

"So w-w-what's new?" he asked.

"If you must know, my car's just been stolen."

"Oh, God, Jill, I'm so sorry." For a moment, he looked almost as devastated as I felt. Grief over the loss of property was something we could share.

I sat down across from him, intending not to say another word about it, but I couldn't stop myself. "Dad, I don't know what I'm going to do. I need a car. Without one, I can't go to college." I shut my eyes and took a deep breath. "Did Mom tell you I got into college? A really top-notch art school. I got a scholarship and everything. Oh, God, Dad, please, could you loan me some money for a car? I swear I'll pay you back."

"Look at me, Jill. You've seen the way I live. I have nothing."

"Dad, I'm only asking for a couple hundred dollars. I know you have lots of money. I know Grandma left you a bundle."

"Who told you that? Did your mother tell you that?" He whacked the table. Tang sloshed out of his glass. "I have nothing!"

"Don't make me beg," I said. I slid my hand across the pink Formica and rested it on his white wrist. My father and I never touched. You could see the poor man wanted to withdraw his arm from the sheer improbability of my act.

"I-I-I can't, Jilly," he said, shaking his head.

I knew then that he honestly couldn't. To ask him to part with his money was like asking another man to part with his sight. I knew I should leave him alone. Instead, I said, "You cheap son of a bitch bastard, just loan me the fucking money!"

Rocking in his chair, he began talking about me in the third person. He addressed the Tang glasses, the daisy stickums, the interminably wafting saloon doors. "What does that daughter of mine want from me? Does she think I'm made of money? Does she and her queen-bee mother think every day's a free lunch? She wants the money? I'll loan her the fucking money.

But with interest. I'll teach that good-for-nothing daughter of mine a little responsibility in this life."

I got up, exploded through the saloon doors, and strode into my mother's room. I lay down on her bed and clamped a pillow over my ears.

But his voice leaked through the stuffing: "Let the bitch walk to her fancy-schmancy art school. Let Miss Hoity-toity take a fucking bus. Let her get a fucking job. If that irresponsible daughter of mine expects me to take care of her all her life, she's got a whole nother think coming."

I've read about the boy who wakes up in his warm bed, only to find himself drenched in another's blood, or the son who comes to in the master bathroom, his hands still clenched around his mother's limp throat after turning her off like a dripping faucet.

Next thing I knew, I had a belt around my dad's neck. Actually, it wasn't a belt. It was a wraparound leather thong my mother used to cinch her new toga dress. And I was pulling, as much to silence my father as to kill him.

They say in times of intense crisis, your soul flees your body and watches you from a safe distance, a corner of the ceiling, say, but not mine. My soul was right there behind my blank eyes and stunned visage. Mostly, I was amazed at how long my father could hold his breath.

I kept expecting him to grab my wrists and yank me off, but he foolishly went after the belt, trying to squeeze his thick fingers between the pinching leather and his red throat. He didn't particularly struggle, no flailing arms or kicking feet, no jarring bucks of his formidable weight. And save for his guttural whimpers and my clenched grunts, we both worked in awful silence.

Jack appeared in the doorway, did a double take, grabbed hold of my wrists, and set my father free.

Dad spilled onto the linoleum, landing on all fours, panting for breath. For a moment, no one said or did anything. My father looked up at me in total bewilderment.

Then the oddest thing happened; without conspiring, without so much as a word being spoken, we all agreed to pretend that I'd never tried to kill him.

My father sat up, shook his red face, and said, "I must have fallen." Jack hauled him back onto the chair, then fetched him a drink of water. My dad downed it like a man who'd been lost in a desert.

I pocketed the leather thong and watched us as if through the wrong end of a telescope—an infinitesimal dad with his two distant children. Sun poured in through the sliding glass doors. The love beads cast prismatic pinwheels and the daisy stickums glowed daisy yellow, and I felt a forlornness I'd never before experienced—and never have since.

I walked out onto the patio, shutting the door behind me. I glanced back, but the glare of the sun turned the glass opaque. It didn't matter. I fully intended never to see that man again.

Oedipus was the saddest of murderers. To hold your father's life in your hands is finally to know a power and pathos that is otherworldly. Oedipus attacked his pop over an insult, too. Galloping toward Thebes one afternoon, Oedipus came across Laius in a chariot. The road was too narrow for them both to squeeze past, and the old man—cantankerous, haughty, obtuse—addressed the boy as if he were a bug, demanding Oedipus step aside. When Oedipus refused, they went at each other like two gunslingers trying to pass on a one-horse bridge, like two motorists shooting each other over a parking spot, like two housewives clubbing each other over the last box of Tide during a Green Light special at K Mart.

Or that's what the Greek chorus—gossips, really—would have you believe.

But I think Oedipus killed Laius because years before the old man had abandoned him on a mountainside, left his baby under the hot sun, in the ceaseless wind, to blow away like a soiled paper plate after a picnic.

Within a week, my mother managed to beg, borrow, and steal the money for a car, as I knew she would, had always known she would, even as I was trying to squeeze the life's breath out of my father.

This time I opted for a more sensible model, a Volkswagen like Arnold's. It had a Tinkertoy engine and I could chug to college on a thimbleful of gas.

I started classes one month later.

The campus was in the high desert, thirty miles north of Los Angeles. To get there, you had to drive through the Tehachapi Pass, a canyon so blustery, Winnebegos were verboten and two-ton tankers shivered like silver leaves. My tiny VW rattled and bucked. Each time the wind gusted, it skipped across the gravelly lanes like a needle skips across a dusty record. At the steepest grade, the poor thing wheezed like an asthmatic.

Classes were held in a sterile, winged building on top of a mountain. Rumor had it that the building was designed so that if the college ever went bankrupt, it could immediately be converted into a hospital.

The neighboring town, a hodgepodge of trailer parks, was filled with working stiffs and retired marines who resented the longhaired unisex art students performing "happenings" at the local police station. (During one performance, a student described the Mona Lisa to a police artist and had an APB put out on her.)

I bought into this new concept of making art out of ideas.

The notion that craft, with its never-good-enough results—a muddy painting, a listing sculpture—could be flashed away until only the pureness of thought remained bordered on religion. I believed and I didn't believe. My education was so lacking that often I hadn't the slightest idea what was going on in class. I hid my ignorance in haughty bravado and took only the most esoteric subjects. I studied linguistics before I knew what a sentence was. I studied deconstruction before I assembled a view of the world. I attended only art survey courses that jump-started in 1960. I pretended the age-old paintings and frescoes I loved were well crafted but irrelevant. I brandished my new savoir-faire attitude like an old-fashioned coed flaunts her big letterman's jacket. But at night, alone with my fears of inadequacy, I studied like a medical student. I committed to memory whole tomes of art history. I dissected every slippery concept—conceptualism, postminimalism, scatter works, and body art—until I got to its heart, or at least to the spot where a heart should have been. I even had Arnold type my freshman term papers.

That fall, we saw each other every chance we could get, mostly in the evenings at his studio. But sometimes our brief assignations took place at Bob's Big Boy, or Four-and-Twenty Pies, or a deserted beach, or a park no wider than a bowling alley that edged Santa Monica Boulevard. We were discreet and we weren't discreet. I couldn't imagine how he explained his absences to his wife, and I didn't ask.

In December, we went away together. It was only a week, but once I'd spent an entire night with him, nothing less would do. Sometimes I think sleep, with its abject vulnerability and careening visions, is a far more intimate act to share than sex. I spent hours watching him dream, his eyes, under papery lids, rolling to zones where I yearned to follow. When I caressed him—I couldn't stop caressing him—my touch became as proprietary as it was tender.

We traveled from motel to boggy motel, each a damp block or two from the gray Pacific. Most of the rooms had yellow blinds or yellow curtains, a trick to make the weary traveler believe every morning is filled with sunny skies and bright hopes. I cried mostly at dawn, shut in the bathroom, a nubby towel monogrammed with CARMEL HOLIDAY or JOLLY ROGER'S INN crushed against my eyes, while Arnold stood outside the locked door, on the cold linoleum, asking what was wrong. We both knew. I couldn't bear his being married any longer.

One morning, after a particularly melodramatic jag of tears, I came out of the bathroom and found him standing by the window. He looked exhausted, having spent most of the night trying to comfort me. It was 5:00, maybe 6:00 A.M. The room was suffused in red, save for the yellow blinds. They cast an especially false, garish light. He had wrapped himself in a pilled pink bedspread. His hair wasn't combed and the coarse gray, far thicker than the fine black, spiked out in all directions. His eyeglasses stood abandoned on the nightstand and he seemed totally lost, a middle-aged man watching the day break or the world end in a gaudy yellow flash, and I knew then that there was no one I would ever love more.

On the drive home, I was unusually quiet. But now and again, like a dead radio that crackles to life, I rose to full volume, wanting to know why he couldn't leave his wife, why he couldn't live with me. I knew he loved me. I knew he couldn't be apart from me any more than I could bear to be apart from him. I didn't understand what he was waiting for.

For the umpteenth time, he tried to explain the complications of a twenty-six-year-old marriage, the history involved, the sheer entanglement of lives. I didn't get it. At eighteen, nothing seemed that complicated to me. After all, I had tossed away my father, so why couldn't he abandon his wife?

When he dropped me off, he explained that he had to spend the holidays with his family. He had no choice.

I said I just wanted him to find a way to unhitch himself. I didn't care about moronic holidays; they were just arbitrary dates pumped up and made glitzy by American capitalism.

On Christmas Day, I cried like an abandoned suburban housewife; on New Year's Eve, like a schoolgirl who'd been stood up for the prom.

Next day, I went to his studio. He was sitting on his cot, elbow on knees, head in hands. He looked spent. He hadn't even bothered to change into his painting pants. They sat on a chair, stiff and dried out. The old layers of paint were so thickly caked on, the material actually held the shape of him, an effigy of air. I lay down beside him and mashed my brow against his thigh. He ran his hand over my face, nape, throat, breast.

"This is just as intolerable for me as it is for you," he said.

We took counsel and tried to figure out what we could do. It was apparent to both of us that our love wasn't going to end anytime soon. Around dusk, I grew despondent again and he tried to make light of things, but his hilarity sounded like a scream from a cage.

Two weeks later, he left his wife and we moved in together. When I told my mom, she got a migraine that lasted four days. Arnold and I rented a hillside bungalow, halfway between his studio and Cal Arts. The bungalow came with modular furniture and was cantilevered over a freeway. During morning rush hour, the kitchen floor shook and the surface of our coffee pitched and sloshed. Sometimes, late at night, lying beside Arnold, the ceaseless whoosh of tires sounded like a wave that never reaches shore. On the weekends, his two hulking teenage children came to visit, and I finally glimpsed fatherhood from the other side.

But that's another story.

———+———

Over the next four years, every weekday morning, Arnold went to his studio while I drove to Cal Arts on the concrete overpasses that traverse the valley. I whizzed past efficiency apartments, vacant lots, gum-snapping gang girls, giving them no more thought than if I'd been rolling over wind-flattened weeds along an emergency lane.

I learned to don the spots and stripes of an avant-garde art student. I mastered the craft of ambiguity, of speech so cryptic that it made my ears buzz, of art for adulation's sake, of dismissing with an irritated sigh all the sentimentality of the world. I scoffed at any dolt for whom art was a tug on the heart. But in dismissing sentiment along with sentimentality, I threw away what I had once worshiped. I tossed out the mystery of art like you toss away a maudlin keepsake.

After all, to join the exclusive ranks of the avant-garde is the quickest way in this world to up your class without money.

Only now and again did I get a shocking peek at the cost.

One afternoon, I was over at a friend's dormitory room when she insisted I watch this "totally weird" man give the stock and futures report on cable TV. Evidently, the old guy and I shared a last name and my friend, who was thinking about using a clip of him in a video piece, wondered if we could be distant relatives. When she snapped on the TV and my father's jowly, blanched face filled the screen, she made a couple of glib cracks. Had it been anyone else's father, I would have laughed, too. Made my own jokes, in fact. But it was my father. And I could see how hard he was working, how hard he tried not to stammer, to get every stock right on the ceaseless ribbon of ticker tape. He didn't look into the camera, but nervously away, just as I do when I'm faced with a lens. No one had clipped his bushy eyebrows in years and they crawled up his humongous forehead. His top lip perspired and he kept wiping it off with the heel of his hand. His eyes registered no emotion save fear.

For a couple of minutes, I just sat there, too stunned to speak. But I was furious as well. Not out of loyalty to my dad. After all, we hadn't spoken to one another since I'd tried to strangle him. It's just that I didn't want my father's plight—this unloved and unlovable man—used as a snappy punch line, a caustic wink to the in crowd.

Then there was the time I was leafing through an art magazine in the college library and came across my dad's apartment building, the Montego Arms, featured in that slick photo essay on LA. The cardboard-brown facade. The orange sofa facing the blank TV. The caption that summed it all up, "The Living Dead."

By the time my brothers showed me the *Time* magazine article about "heart attack personalities" that featured him, I barely had an iota of rancor left for the man. I read about my dad, the quintessential type A personality, as you read another father's long-lost diary—a man who must interrupt every conversation, a man who clenches his fist and pounds the table for emphasis, a man who explodes over trivia, a man who waits in stalled traffic like another man waits beside a ticking bomb. I studied the photograph. My father looked terrified laid out on the doctor's white examining table like a corpse on a marble slab. I knew he saw his own death.

I stumbled upon my father only one other time during the years we didn't speak. It was in the late spring of 1975. I had just graduated from college. My future seemed bright and limitless. I was living with Arnold, I had a spanking-new bachelor of fine arts diploma, and nothing could stop me. (I hadn't a clue of what snares awaited—doubts, disillusionments, sorrows, deaths.) At that moment, my world was tinged in the pastel colors of the Galleria Mall. Arnold and I were waiting in line at the movies when I spied my dad near the planters. He was wearing a canary yellow leisure suit. I didn't want Arnold to know I'd seen him, God forbid have to introduce them. I'd barely told Arnold anything about my dad. The queue began shuffling toward the theater doors. I told Arnold to go ahead, that I'd catch up with him inside.

Then, keeping a discreet distance, I dogged my father.

He had wandered over to another planter and was eyeing a spider fern. With great tenderness, he stroked the fern's oily frond as if it were a human hand. Then he stooped over and examined its roots. We were on the mezzanine, under the mall's gala light-sculpture—a whirling orange-and-purple globe. My father looked terribly nervous. Suddenly, I had an insatiable yearning to approach him, tap him on the shoulder, and tell him not to worry. He began rummaging through his shopping bag. I couldn't imagine what was inside. My father never bought anything, ever. Taking a surreptitious glance around, he dug out a scissors, grabbed the fern by its shaft, and snipped off a cutting. I did a double take. My father was helping himself to mall plants. I watched him filch a cactus bud, another fern frond, and something viridescent and prickly. All the while, I ached to make contact, to talk to him, say something.

I didn't. I kept my heart in check.

When the harvesting was over, he stepped onto the escalator and descended into the crowd. The mall was jam-packed with harried moms and cranky children. I watched him plod his way past the families until he become a yellow speck and was lost to me.

PART

FOUR

March 6/86

Dear Jill:

I thought it would be nice to touch base with you as it has been quite awhile + we all kind of reminisce about former times. I still remember the good times we had at our homes both in Rancho del Sol and Encino. I still remember the crazy stories you used to tell us about your experiences at school. I still remember you getting mad at some drawing you would be doing + tearing it up—making us all laugh. So when you think back, there is always something pleasant to remember.

Whenever I speak to your mother, I hear a fair amount about you, your life + achievements. I followed with interest your giving up a painting career + creating a career in writing—how you would practically lock yourself up to concentrate completely on your work. As I understand it, your first book has been accepted—not by a fly-by-night-type publisher, but one of quality. This is great. I could say I'm proud of you, the standard cliché—however, I'd rather say I'm proud of both of us—you for doing what you've done + me, even though it was quite a time

201

ago, for instilling some kind of work habit + discipline into you, in my own way, that I hope makes you what you are.

Sure, I don't get a chance to see my kids (we're all very busy), but I know this much—my children turned out pretty damn good in their own way. Someday we'll have a chance to talk about this.

As to things here at home in the valley, I've become a commodity broker. I had hoped to retire a few years ago, but the market is so bad, Jill, I've lost practically everything. Why, oh why didn't I get out when I could? I keep very active with my new hobby of growing + cultivating Japanese bonsai trees. I'm sure you've seen exhibitions of these dwarf trees in tiny urns. I have a collection of over a hundred. And so, if I feel like taking a break from reading the commodity reports, I've always got some pruning or wiring to do on my trees.

I'm diabetic now + neuropathy has set in. There's nothing one can do about it. I've lost a lot of feeling in my legs + some feeling in my fingers. If I stub my toe or accidentally put my feet into boiling water, I don't feel anything. Sometimes my toes swell up to the size of link sausages. I'm on insulin, but the only real thing is for me to control my sugar intake, which is easier said than done.

Well, this kind of brings you up-to-date with me. Jill when you get a chance, I sure would like to hear from you, letting me know your accomplishments + a little about life for you in New York, as your mother said you've moved there again, and, of course, that's where my letter has found you.

Love

Dad

I hadn't heard from my father in fifteen years, hadn't seen him since I'd glimpsed him in the mall. I read the letter with befuddled intensity. First, to take it in—the beige paper, the blue ink, the stumbling handwriting that held within its pinched loops a ghost of my own enigmatic scrawl. Then to see if underlying a simple phrase—"I thought it would be nice to touch base with you"—there was a clue of why, now, after a decade and a half, he'd written. I recognized whole phrases he must have borrowed from my mother's phone calls "your first book has been accepted—*not by a fly-by-night-type publisher, but one of quality.*" Mom had long ago remarried, but I knew she spoke to him once in a blue moon to brag about her kids. I knew that during the time he heard my mother's voice, officious and boastful, his children were alive to him, if only in the fleeting rush of my mother's enthusiasm.

I showed the letter to Arnold, then stood over his shoulder as he read it. Where I saw impregnable mystery, the miffs of family history, even a tincture of subterfuge, Arnold saw a simple letter by an extremely lonely father. We were sitting in our kitchen, an elbow of living space in a big, dark loft in lower Manhattan. Arnold painted in the one room; I wrote in the other. It was our third sublet in as many years. Even at high noon, there wasn't enough daylight to read by. When I complained to the woman who'd rented us the loft, she said she'd gone to a hypnotist and had ridded herself of her need for light.

I phoned Jack that weekend. He was living in Portland, Oregon, teaching neuroscience at the university. Evidently, he'd also gotten a letter from our father. (Dad must have sat down and written all his children in one go.) Jack didn't find it as peculiar as I did. He'd been in touch with Dad. Once a year or so, he called him.

I asked if Dad was happy to hear from him.

"It's hard to say, Jill. The guy doesn't exactly emote. For the first couple of minutes, he seems genuinely excited, then . . . well, you can sense he just wants to get off the line."

I wrote my father that afternoon, an oddly cheery reply. I said I was happy to hear from him, then underlined the word *happy*. I said I was touched that he'd written, then underlined *touched*. (I was deeply touched. Whenever I pictured my dad— colossal forehead, frightened gray eyes—bent over the four letters to his four children, a tug of subterranean sadness pulled me under.) I said that I, too, thought about him. I tried to conjure up a few fond memories to match his examples. I said I remembered him working in his garden, his truly magnificent rose garden, and how he instilled his love of nature into us children. I said I appreciated his being a . . . a noninterferring father who let us kids find our own way.

I added that I knew we'd had our bad times, worse than bad, but from here on in, we should try to rekindle our relationship, keep in touch, not let years pass without writing or phoning. I said I very much missed him, that our having a relationship meant a great deal to me. I signed my letter "With love." I doubt he understood my one or two unnecessary digs, but I'll never know for certain.

The guy never wrote back.

Six months later, Jack phoned to tell me that our father had had an accident, that he'd fallen off a ladder while pruning a tree, a life-size tree, and cracked his head on the cement patio. He was conscious and alert now, but there was definitely brain damage.

"Is he going to be okay? Can he walk and talk?"

"He has a bad concussion. The good news is that his motor and speech skills don't seem to be affected. The bad news is that he really smashed his forehead. If there's any permanent brain damage, it's going to be in the prefrontal area; it may affect his personality. I don't have a clear clinical picture yet, but he seems okay. I just got off the phone with him."

"And?"

"And . . . who can tell, Jill. He's frightened and extremely agitated, but that's how he always sounds, so it's hard to say. His condition's stable. The fall happened a few days ago. They're keeping him in the hospital one more night, then sending him home. Do you want his phone number?"

I picked at a fleck of dust gummed between the phone's push buttons. "I guess," I said at length.

That afternoon, I called my father. It took him a fumbling minute to haul the receiver to his ear.

"H-h-hello?" His voice sounded infinitesimal.

"Hey, it's me, Dad, Jill."

"Who?"

"Your daughter, Jill."

"Jill?"

"Yep."

"Oh, God, Jill, I'm a hydrocephalic now. I have water on the brain."

"I'm sure it's temporary, Dad."

"No, no. The doctor's said it's irreversible. I'm finished, Jill."

I hadn't spoken to the guy in fifteen years. I didn't know what to say. "You sound good," I lied.

"I must have tripped on the ladder. It's my diabetic neuropathy. I hope you're watching your sugar intake, Jill. I can't feel my feet anymore. It's like having someone else's feet on the end of my legs." I heard the rattle of a cart, the whoosh of curtains. "The nurse is here. I have to go now."

Click.

For a moment, I just stood there, holding the dead receiver in my hand. Arnold was out. I'd asked him to leave for a while so I could talk to my dad in private. It was rush hour, but I could barely hear the rumble of traffic, the jimjam of horns. Our loft was in a cavernous alley. Our scant windows faced the gray marble bricks of the Family Court building. Only at dusk, in high summer, during a fleeting tilt of the earth, did a faint spoke of sunlight bounce off the gray bricks and spill onto our floor. I sat down in the tepid glow. While you couldn't read by it, at least you knew there was a world out there.

———†———

My father's health rapidly declined after the fall. Or at least that's what my brothers told me. A stutterer by nature, he now spoke in halting "ahs," repeated ad infinitum, pauses trapped in breath like bubbles in glass. When he stubbed a toe, he forgot to soak it—a serious mishap for a diabetic. He almost lost his foot on two occasions. His peripheral vision degenerated and the edges of his world folded closed. The blood couldn't get to his eyes, his hands, his feet. His heart couldn't pump it. His sugar-laden veins were collapsing like paper straws.

His brokerage firm had to let him go. Even his most loyal clients had abandoned him. Let's face it, who wants a brain-damaged stockbroker?

I called him now and again—twice, maybe three times that year. Our conversations were excruciating. Or perhaps it was only the memory of our conversations that were excruciating. While my dad and I talked on the phone, we were painfully shy, almost kind to each other. If he lurched off onto a verbal rampage, I parried it with a joke. Only afterward, when I hung up and picked over the long pauses, did our awkwardness transmogrify into insufferability.

That summer, he had a heart attack, followed by another, fiercer one. He was working the commodity floor when the jolt struck. (He still traded a smidgen in futures.) My father ignored the pain and kept going. The ache must have been intolerable. For the better part of the day, he actually traded and bellowed and bargained while a hunk of his heart dried up like meat left on an open counter.

That evening, he was rushed to intensive care. My brothers and I, scattered all over the country, agreed to stagger our visits so that one of us could be with him at all times. I think we were stunned by our paternal dutifulness.

When my turn came, I flew to LA, rented a car, chugged through jammed streets, parked in a colossal tiered structure with columns thicker than the Parthenon's, then wandered the icy corridors of a pastel-colored hospital, only to find my dad sitting up in bed, frenetically hammering the tiny remote control to his TV set against a metal meal tray. The tray pinged and leapt. Orange juice sloshed over the rim of a glass. My dad looked flushed and blanched at the same time, as if all the blood in his head had puddled in a few spots—neck, hairline, ears. He was shouting for a nurse, railing about why a goddamn hospital that cost a goddamn fortune couldn't get him a goddamn TV that worked. When he saw me, he stopped, blinked, then sank back into the sheets.

My dad had never seen me as an adult. I wasn't sure he recognized me.

I walked over to the bed. His face—wrinkled, scaly, sweaty—as foreign and familiar to me as the underside of my own feet, lay on the pillow before me.

Despite a tinge of revulsion, I kissed his brow.

"Hey, how you doing?" I asked.

"Oh, oh, Jill," he said, squinting up at me. "It's so good to see you."

"Good to see you, too, Dad," I said.

"My TV isn't working, Jill. I don't understand why they can't fix one goddamn TV."

"I'll check into it later."

"Could you do it now?"

I knew if I didn't do it right then, he'd be unable to think about anything else.

I spoke to the nurse. She brushed off my dad's complaint with a heavenward roll of her eyes. "He's at it again. Your dad's quite a card." For a moment, I thought maybe she had the wrong father—I'd just passed dozens of rooms filled with fathers, all as chalky and fragile as my own. She pulled out my dad's chart and explained his condition—huffing ventricles, jammed veins, a myocardial infarction in the left coronary artery. I missed a few technical details, but I got the general gist; without open-heart surgery, my dad's prognosis was nil, and he was too befuddled and obstinate and frightened to make a decision.

I asked for a pencil and paper, then went back to his room.

"Are they going to fix my TV?"

"In a while," I said.

"I can't lay here all day without a goddamn TV—"

"Forget the fucking TV, Dad, and listen. Did they explain the surgery to you?"

He waved away the surgery, then rolled on his side. "I-I-I don't want to know."

"Well, you're going to have to know, Dad." I perched on the edge of his bed and picked up the pencil. "This is your heart," I said. With dire concentration, I tried to draw my father's heart. For a moment, I envisioned all the hearts I'd ever seen—cardboard chocolate-box hearts, Hallmark Valentine's Day hearts, the *I Love Lucy* pillowed heart, the pounding organ I watched on TV documentaries. And still I had no idea what this man's heart could possibly look like.

I drew the most rudimentary, school primer rendition of a heart.

"You could always draw so well," he said, barely glancing at my sketch. "I remember when you were a little girl, you'd always be drawing. You'd show your mother and me a picture of a horse or a house or something, and when we'd praise it, you'd rip it up, saying *you* didn't think it was any good."

I laughed, but apparently he saw no humor in this. So I sketched the left ventricle facing the valves.

"Had this wall died, Dad, there'd be no point in operating. The good news is, it's still alive."

He took the good news indifferently.

"If they replace the arteries here"—I sketched what I imagined arteries looked like, sink pipes spouting from a cartoon heart—"the blood will start flowing and—"

"Should I even bother, Jill? Maybe it would be better if I died. What would you do?"

"I'd have the operation, and if I didn't like the way things turned out, I could always kill myself afterward."

He gave this some thought. "That's good advice," he said. "Thanks."

"You're welcome."

I found someone to fix his TV, then sat with him till he fell asleep in the TV's jittery light. Before I left, I pocketed the drawing. I didn't want an illustration of his failing heart lying around for him to find later. But, once outside the hospital, and even after I got back to New York, I still didn't chuck it. I kept it as a talisman to help him through his surgery. After all, in my drawing, everything turned out okay in the end.

My father survived the operation, but just barely. He never regained his strength and wound up in a nursing home. He died six months later.

Last year, I found the drawing crumpled in the back of a file drawer, under a pile of manuscripts. Studying it, I came as close to genuine grief as I ever felt for my dad. I didn't weep or miss him, but my own little cartoon heart was pounding.

ABOUT THE AUTHOR

Jill Ciment is the author of *Small Claims* and *The Law of Falling Bodies*. She has received grants from the National Endowment for the Arts and the New York State Foundation for the Arts. She teaches creative writing at Columbia University and Rutgers University and lives in New York City.